Evolution of the Danish Population
from 1835 to 2000

Evolution of the Danish Population from 1835 to 2000

Kirill F. Andreev

Monographs on Population Aging, 9.

Odense University Press

Evolution of the Danish Population
from 1835 to 2000
© Kirill F. Andreev and University Press of Southern Denmark, 2002
Printed by Special-Trykkeriet Viborg a-s, Denmark
Cover illustration: Herbs growing on the mountain of the two lovers.
Paper-cut by Sonia Brandes.
ISBN 87-7838-716-7
ISSN 0909-119X

University Press of Southern Denmark
Campusvej 55
DK-5230 Odense M
Phone +45 66 15 79 99 - Fax +45 66 15 81 26
E-mail: Press@forlag.sdu.dk
Internet bookstore: www.universitypress.dk

Table of contents

Table of contents 5
List of tables 6
List of figures 7
Author 8
Acknowledgements 9
1. Introduction 11
2. Construction of the Danish mortality database 13
   2.1   Introduction 13
   2.2   Danish demographic statistics 13
   2.3   Database structure 16
   2.4   Original data 18
      2.4.1 Population 18
      2.4.2 Deaths 18
   2.5   Construction of the database 19
      2.5.1 Deaths 19
         Age zero 22
         Ages 100+ 22
         Distribution of deaths by Lexis triangles 23
      2.5.2 Population 24
         Extinct cohort population 28
         Population at exact age 30
3. A descriptive analysis of the evolution of the Danish population
with focus on mortality 31
   3.1   Danish population changes over the period 1835–2000 31
   3.2   The Danish mortality evolution 38
      3.2.1 Life expectancy at birth 38
      3.2.2 Period survivorship 40
      3.2.3 Mortality 41
      3.2.4 Rates of mortality changes over time 50
      3.2.5 Sex ratio of mortality 52
      3.2.6 Compression of mortality 55
4. A comparison of mortality in Denmark and other developed countries 63
   4.1   Introduction 63
   4.2   Denmark to Sweden 63

4.3	Denmark to Norway	66
4.4	Denmark to Finland	69
4.5	Denmark to the Netherlands	71
4.6	Denmark to Austria	71
4.7	Denmark to France	74
4.8	Denmark to England and Wales	76
4.9	Denmark to Japan	78
4.10	Denmark to Canada	80
4.11	Concluding notes	82
5. Cause-specific mortality		87
5.1	An analysis of cause-specific mortality	87
5.2	Time trends in cause-specific mortality	94
6. Conclusions and further research		105
6.1	Main results	105
6.2	Further research	107
References		111
Appendix		115
Odense Monographs on Population Aging		124

List of tables

2.1	The death distribution within the age group 95–99 and in the year 1916 and 1921–1940	21
2.2	The number of deaths above age 100	23
3.1	Annual gains in Danish life expectancy in the selected periods	39
3.2	Life expectancy in the beginning of the 20th century	50
3.3	Proportions of the life table deaths in Denmark	58
5.1	Decomposition of excess Danish mortality by causes of death for the period 1985–1993	90
5.2	Decomposition of excess Danish mortality by aggregated causes of death for the period 1985–1993	94

List of figures

2.1	Illustration of the Danish database structure with Lexis diagram	17
2.2	Deviation between the original and the redistributed populations	29
3.1	Changes in the Danish population from 1835 till 2000	32
3.2	Changes in the age structure of the Danish population	32
3.3	Danish population distribution	34
3.4	Ratio of the Danish population distribution to the average levels in 1835–1920	35
3.5	Cumulative growth rate of the Danish population	37
3.6	Danish life expectancy at birth	39
3.7	Danish survivorship by single calendar year	42
3.8	Danish death rates	43
3.9	Rate of Danish mortality changes over time	54
3.10	Sex ratio of Danish mortality	55
3.11	Danish life table death distribution	57
3.12	Entropy of Danish life table death distribution	60
4.1	Ratio of death rates, Denmark to Sweden	65
4.2	Ratio of death rates, Denmark to Norway	68
4.3	Ratio of death rates, Denmark to Finland	70
4.4	Ratio of death rates, Denmark to the Netherlands	72
4.5	Ratio of death rates, Denmark to Austria	73
4.6	Ratio of death rates, Denmark to France	75
4.7	Ratio of death rates, Denmark to England and Wales	77
4.8	Ratio of death rates, Denmark to Japan	79
4.9	Ratio of death rates, Denmark to Canada	81
4.10	The highest death rates in Denmark compared with other countries	85
4.11	The lowest death rates in Denmark compared with other countries	85
5.1(a)	Disadvantageous trends in Danish cause-specific mortality. Males.	96
5.1(b)	Disadvantageous trends in Danish cause-specific mortality. Females	100
6.1	Annual consumption of alcohol (population aged 15 and over)	109
6.2	Annual consumption of tobacco (population aged 15 and over)	109

Note that most of the Lexis maps are available in color on the accompanying CD-ROM.

Author

Kirill F. Andreev
Department of Community Health & Epidemiology
Abramsky Hall
Queen's University
Kingston, Ontario
Canada K7L 3N6
Home page: http://post.queensu.ca/~andreevk/
E-mail: andreevk@post.queensu.ca
E-mail: kirill_andreev@hotmail.com

Acknowledgements

I am grateful to James W. Vaupel and Bernard Jeune for promoting my work on this project. I wish also to thank Anatoli Yashin, Väinö Kannisto, Roger Thatcher, Shiro Horiuchi, Hans Chr. Johansen, Vladimir Shkolnikov, Ivan Iachine, Michael Bubenheim for numerous discussions of demographic problems; John Wilmoth, Hans Lundström, Axel Skytthe, Dorthe Larsen, Otto Andersen, Michael Væth, Jacques Vallin, Thomas Burch, Ewa Tabeau, Frans Willikens, Jens-Kristian Borgan, Nico Keilman, Kirsten Enger Dybendal, Timo Nikander, Alexia Fürnkranz-Prskawetz, Alexander Hanika, Steve Smallwood and Dimiter Philipov for making available mortality data.

I am grateful to Kirsten M. Gauthier for help with book layout and Sigrid Gellers-Barkmann for help with data acquisition and preparation. I also extend my thanks to the entire staff of the Max Planck Institute for Demographic Research and of the University of Southern Denmark for their overall support of this project. The project has been completed at Queen's University, Canada with kindly support of Samuel Shortt and Boris Sobolev.

This research was supported in part by grants from the U.S. National Institute on Aging (P01-08761), the Danish Research Councils and the Max Planck Institute for Demographic Research.

1. Introduction

We have the 17th-century parish registrars and their far-sighted collection of statistical data – which has been carried on to the present day by government statisticians – to thank for the fact that we are now in a position to study different aspects of the human life span. One of the major topics in demographic research is the continuing mortality decline in European countries. Although many researchers have been studying the mortality transition of the last two centuries in Europe, "our understanding of historical mortality patterns, and of their causes and implications, is still in its infancy" (Schofield and Reher, 1991).

Research in this area is usually hampered by the lack of reliable long-term mortality series. Danish population statistics, which embody an enormous amount of relevant data extending well back into the seventieth century, are an important exception. One of the outstanding features of the Danish statistics is that one can use them to reconstruct the mortality evolution by a single age, year and cohort. By studying age-specific and cohort-specific mortality trends rather than by simply using the crude mortality indicators, deeper insights into the nature of mortality development can be gained.

Chapter 2 is devoted to the authoritative account of the construction of the Danish mortality database. In this chapter, I bring together all sources of original information on Danish population and provide a brief description of the history of Danish population statistics. Estimation of Danish death rates over age and time can not be carried out by solely using the official published population data. For example, in the 19th century population estimates for years between censuses are not available and deaths are aggregated into 5-year age groups. Moreover, population estimates at the highest ages are not always given up to the last age attained rather they are published as open age aggregates, i.e. 90 and over. Estimation of death rates can still be accomplished if missing population estimates are produced and adjustment of original data to the desired level of detail is carried out by special methods. A description of such methods is also included in Chapter 2.

The subject of the next chapter is a descriptive analysis of the evolution of the Danish population since 1835. The chapter includes an investigation of changes in the Danish population structure with an emphasis on population aging, an analysis of trends in death rates over age and time, an exploration of rates of mortality decline, an examination of compression of mortality and an investigation of male-female differences in survival. Most of the findings are provided in great details and the results are presented with the help of the Lexis map techniques (Caselli et al., 1985; Caselli et al., 1987; Vaupel et al., 1998).

Chapter 4 includes the results of a comparison of Danish mortality with death rates in other countries. Nine countries (Sweden, Norway, Finland, the Netherlands, France, England and Wales, Austria, Canada and Japan) have been selected for comparison with Denmark. All of them have a long history of reliable population statistics and comparable statistical resources. Country specific differences in survival are investigated with the help of mortality ratio surfaces, which are estimated by the single calendar year and single year of age, for all ages from 0 to 99 and for all years where data were available. The analysis clearly revealed age-specific differences in Danish survival and exposed their dynamics over time. Two remarkable findings of this analysis are the unfavorable development in death rates of middle-aged and the excess of Danish mortality compared to other countries in recent decades.

Understanding of the determinants of disadvantageous trends in Danish mortality can be significantly improved by the analysis of causes of deaths. Cause-specific mortality developments over the last three decades in Denmark, Sweden, the Netherlands and Japan have been investigated in Chapter 5. The analysis helped to reveal the causes of deaths, providing the most significant contributions to the excess of Danish mortality in recent years. The trends in the causes of deaths, which are of concern, are also reported and discussed.

The monograph is accompanied by a CD-ROM containing the electronic version of the monograph itself, color and black/white Lexis maps included in the monograph, the trends of the analyzed causes of deaths and the animated graphs of Danish population and mortality changes.

The value of the Danish mortality data is not limited by the analysis conducted in this monograph. The database includes both data on population and deaths and permits an estimation of death rates over age, time and along the cohort lines. For these reasons, the database can be extremely useful for mortality and population projections; for the wide range of epidemiological studies in which the mortality of the Danish population as a whole is compared with the mortality in selected groups of individuals (e.g., Christensen, K. et al., 1995); for studies on the influence of different genes on the human life span where dynamics of gene proportions over age is analyzed (Yashin et al., 1998). In the last case, for example, estimation of relative risks associated with a particular genotype requires mortality estimates for cohorts born a hundred years ago and earlier.

2. Construction of the Danish mortality database

2.1 Introduction

Construction of the Danish mortality database described in this section, has the primary goal of estimating death rates over age and time by single calendar year and by single year of age. Official statistical information necessary for such purpose is available only for recent decades. Proceeding to earlier years, requires the application of non-trivial methods for adaptation of death counts and the production of intercensual population estimates. Section 2.2 provides a brief historical review of Danish population statistics, which is an ultimate source of information underlying this project. Section 2.3 includes the necessary information about the database structure and its coverage. In section 2.4, I discuss the available raw data used for database compilation and section 2.5 brings together the methods that have been used for achieving the desired level of data completeness and aggregation.

2.2 Danish demographic statistics

The Danish population and vital statistics are rooted in the seventeenth century, when parish registers became compulsory. In this section, I list the demographic events relevant to the present work in chronological order. The information presented here is based mostly on publications of Matthiessen (1970) and Impagliazzo (1984). Detailed information on early Danish parish registers can be found in Johansen (1998).

1645–1646 - parish registers of births, deaths and marriages maintained by the clergy became compulsory by rescript. The territory of Denmark was covered only partially in the following few decades.

1735 - summary statistics of parish registers became available annually in the form of a statistical publication called the "General Extract".

1769, August 15th. First census. Census information was presented in summary tables. The population was divided by sex, and age was reported by six groups for the ages under 48 and by an open age class 48+. Marital status was recorded as married and non-married. Occupational status was divided into nine groups. Although the enumerated population was "de jure population", some temporarily absent persons, e.g. sailors, may have been omitted. Some military personnel were also excluded from the enumeration for security reasons.

1775 - A prescribed schedule of vital statistics was introduced. Clergy used this schedule to fill in deaths by sex and 10-year age groups, and births by sex and legitimacy. Starting in 1783, the number of marriages was also included.

1787, July 1st. Second census. This census was similar to that of 1769, with the exception that the names of the individuals were recorded as well.

1796 - The first statistical office (Tabelkontoret) was founded. This office conducted the 1801 census. The office was abolished in 1819 in favor of the statistical commission (Tabelkommisionen).

1800 - Births reported by the clergy were divided into the categories live-births and stillborn.

1801, February 1st. Third census. The population was enumerated by 10-year age groups. Statistical reports of this census were published together with the reports of the 1834 census.

1829 - Introduction of the death certificate.

1834, February 18th. Fourth census. This is the first census conducted by the Tabelkommisionen. The population was enumerated by 10-year age groups. The results of this census were published in the first statistical publication (Tabelværket, 1st series, 1st volume).

1835 - The distribution of marriages by broad age groups was introduced. Deaths became recorded by the following age groups: below 1 year, 1–2 years, 3–4 years, 5–9 years, etc. Such detailed death statistics made possible the calculation of reliable mortality estimates.

1840, February 1st. Fifth census. The population was recorded by five-year age groups and by single age for ages under five. This is the first census in which the population was tabulated by five-year age groups.

1845, February 1st. Sixth census.

1850 - The national statistical office was founded (Statens Statistiske Bureau, later Det Statistiske Department, and presently Danmarks Statistik).

1850, February 1st. Seventh census.

1855, February 1st. Eighth census.

1860, February 1st. Ninth census. The birth distribution by age of mother was introduced.

1864, Autumn. Sønderjylland (hertugdømmet Slesvig) became part of Germany. About 55,000 people emigrated from this region in 1867–1900, the major part to America and a smaller part to Denmark.

1870, February 1st. Tenth census. For the first time the population was reported by single age. The island of Ærø became part of Denmark with the peace treaty of 30 October 1864 and was included in the census statistics.

1877 - Birth certificates were required everywhere in Denmark.

1880, February 1st. Eleventh census.
1890, February 1st. Twelfth census.
1901, February 1st. Thirteenth census.
1906, February 1st. Fourteenth census.
1911, February 1st. Fifteenth census.
1911 - Individual data on birth, marriage and death were sent from clergy to the national statistical office, thereby abolishing the former schedule of vital statistics.
1916, February 1st. Sixteenth census.
1920, June 15th - Sønderjylland (hertugdømmet Slesvig) became part of Denmark, thereby increasing the total population by about 163,000 people (about 5.5%).
1921, February 1st. Seventeenth census.
1925, November 5th. Eighteenth census.
1930, November 5th. Nineteenth census.
1935, November 5th. Twentieth census. In this census, questionnaires were distributed to all individuals.
1940, November 5th. Twenty-first census.
1945, June 15th. Twenty-second census.
1950, November 7th. Twenty-third census.
1955, October 1st. Twenty-fourth census.
1960, September 26th. Twenty-fifth census.
1965, September 27th. Twenty-sixth census.
1968 The Central Population Register (CPR) was established. The process of registering statistical information became continuous. The establishment of the CPR led to the abolishment of the questionnaire-based census.
1970, November 9th. Twenty-seventh census. This is the last census, which used questionnaires.
1976, January 1st. First CPR based census.
1981, January 1st. Second CPR based census.
Information on vital statistics has been published in the Table Works (Statistisk Tabelværker) since the year 1801. The first publication covers the period from 1801 to 1833 and was published together with the 1801 and 1834 censuses. All other publications cover five-year periods. The population statistical report (Befolkningens Bevægelser) has been published since 1931 on an annual basis. This publication includes annual estimates of Danish population and its change over single year due to deaths, migration and births. To complete the review of Danish statistics, I have reproduced the table of former publications of Danish statistics from Befolkningens Bevægelser 1999 in the Appendix Table 1. The most recent publications, e.g.

Befolkningens Bevægelser 1999, are available online and can be downloaded through Danmarks Statistik[1] web site.

Two other sources of population statistics, which are important to mention, include the publication "Dødsårsagerne i Danmark" (Causes of Death in Denmark) issued by the Danish Ministry of Health (Sundhedsstyrelsen, www.sst.dk) and the publication "Befolkningen i kommunerne pr. 1. Januar" (Population by provinces) published by the Danmarks Statistik.

2.3 Database structure

The right choice of database structure can substantially reduce both the cost of data retrieval and the basic computational operations performed on the data. Based on my experience the following database structure is suggested:

COHORT	AGE	POPULATION	DEATHS	TIMING	YEAR
...		Example of records		...	...
1940	30	32,592	13	1	1970
1939	30	31,256	16	2	1970
...	...	...	...	...	...

As the data are collected by years, the database is kept sorted by YEAR, AGE and TIMING, and each year includes the same number of ages, and each age includes two timings or Lexis triangles. The Lexis diagram shown in Fig 2.1 illustrates the rationale for the proposed structure.

The database includes six fields and each record is used to store the information about one Lexis triangle (TIMING). Timing "1" corresponds to the triangle BCD and the timing "2" to the triangle ABD. The column DEATHS contains the number of deaths in these Lexis triangles. For example, in the above given table, 13 deaths occurred in the cohort $z=1940$, year $y=1970$ and age $x=30$. The 16 deaths which occurred in the same year and age, but in the previous cohort $z=1939$, belong to timing 2 (triangle ABD). Consequently, the sum of the deaths in timings 1 and 2 is the number of deaths occurred in the given year and age (rectangle ABCD). The interpretation of numbers stored in the field POPULATION depends on the timing number. If the timing is equal to one, the population at risk at exact age x over period $[y, y+1]$ is recorded, otherwise it is the population on January 1st year y

---

[1] National statistical office of Denmark. Danmarks Statistik, Sejrøgade 11, 2100 København Ø. E-mail: dst@dst.dk. Internet: www.dst.dk.

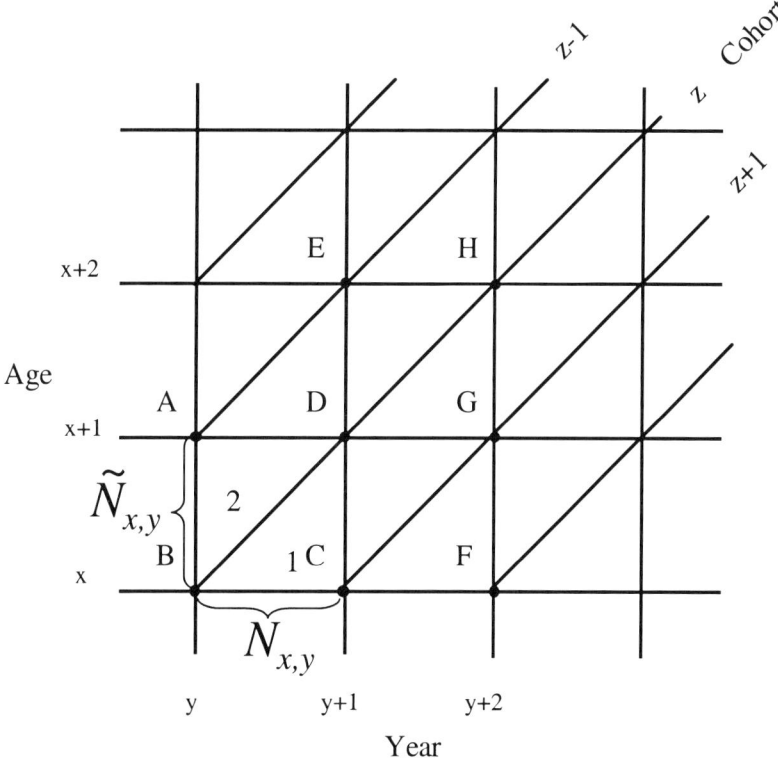

Figure 2.1. Illustration of the Danish database structure with the Lexis diagram

aged [x, $x+1$] that is listed. In our example, the population numbers are depicted by lines BC and BA on the Lexis diagram and equal to 32,592 and 31,256, respectively. The database structure presented here is not optimized for the size. The variables YEAR, COHORT, AGE and TIMING are linearly dependent and we can compute, for examples, the YEAR variable as YEAR = COHORT + AGE + TIMING - 1. In other words, one of these four variables can safely be omitted without any loss of information, but given the importance of all fields and computational conveniences, they are kept in the database intentionally since this permits a significant reduction in the time of computations.

Data stored in such a format can be used for calculations of virtually any demographic indicators: central death rates, period and cohort life tables, rates of mortality changes in time or age directions, et cetera. In addition, the absolute numbers of population estimates and deaths stored in the database permit us to test statistical hypotheses and to construct confidence intervals for the computed values. More detailed discussion of the Lexis diagram can be found in Impagliazzo (1984) and Tabeau et al. (1994). In the latter report, the different observational planes used by the national statistical offices are also discussed. The reader interested in the historical aspects of the development of this diagram may refer to Vandeschrick (2001).

2.4 Original data

2.4.1 Population

Danish population data before 1906, are available only from censuses, which were held every five or ten years. The censuses held in 1801 and 1834, tabulate population by ten-year age groups and those held between 1834 and 1870 by five-year age groups. As of 1870, the population is tabulated by single-age groups, which makes these censuses entirely suitable for our requirements as the population estimates are available with the necessary level of details. The major part of the work on population estimates for the 19th century, therefore, is concentrated on reconstructing the single-age distribution and computing population estimates for the periods between censuses. All Danish censuses in the nineteenth century were dated February 1st, with the only exception in 1834 (February 18th). The database format requires that the population estimates are for January 1st, therefore an additional population adjustment has to be made.

Starting in 1906, population estimates by single year of age are available from Danmarks Statistik. They can be added directly to the database. For the years 1906–1940, the population at higher ages is given by the open age class 85+, leaving the single-age distribution unknown. In this case, the population can be estimated indirectly by the extinct cohort method (Vincent, 1951). Some data uncertainties also exist during the period from 1932 to 1940, as the population estimates available for these years were rounded off to hundreds. Appendix Table 2 summarizes the available raw population statistics.

2.4.2 Deaths

The information about the available data on deaths is included in the Appendix Table 3. The period from 1943 to the present time does not require any additional manipulations – the death counts can be added directly to the database. For the period from 1921 to 1942, the data are available in the same degree of detail, with the exception that deaths for ages above 100 were aggregated into the single-age group 100+. The deaths in this age group have to be separated by a single year of age. The death counts recorded in this group are very small, and the influence of the separation procedure on mortality estimates at lower ages is negligible.

The data become less abundant as we move back to the earlier years. In the period 1916–1920, the death counts are given by single year and age (see Fig. 2.1, rectangle ABCD). Here the death counts have to be split between cohorts in some reasonable way.

In the period 1835–1915, the death counts are given only in five-year age groups. These data have to be separated by a single year of age and afterwards by a cohort to fit the database standard.

2.5   Construction of the database

2.5.1 Deaths

1921–1999
Data on deaths available for these years fit the database structure entirely and were added directly to the database, with the exception of the open age class 100+ for the period 1921–1942. The separation of the 100+ group is discussed below.

1916–1920
Death counts for the years 1916–1920 are given by single year of age. Before adding these data to the database, we needed to separate them between the two cohorts that constitute the Lexis rectangle. I did this by splitting deaths evenly between cohorts at age one and over. This seems to be a reasonable, albeit not a perfect solution at the moment. The separation of cohort deaths at age zero can be achieved more satisfactorily, because more detailed statistics are available for this age. The procedure, which I applied to all years where it was possible, is described below.

1911–1915
Deaths for the years 1911–1915 were published by five-year age groups. Along with the death counts given by single year, the aggregated death counts for years 1911–1915 were published by single year of age. The available single-year-of-age death distribution was used to allocate deaths by single age from 1911 to 1915. Subsequently the death counts were split evenly between the cohorts.

1835–1910
The deaths for this period are aggregated by five-year age groups, which must be then separated by the single year of age. As the main intention was to stick to the original data as closely as possible, I selected interpolation as the proper tool for carrying out this task. By using interpolation instead of statistical graduation techniques, we can store the death counts in the Lexis triangles bound to the five-year totals published in the official statistics. In order to obtain the original

aggregated data, one can simply sum up the death counts in the Lexis triangles constituting the age group. Naturally, the annual series of the total number of deaths computed from the database will coincide with the total number of deaths found in the official statistics.

Before proceeding to the interpolation, an appropriate interpolation method must be selected and its suitability for the problem tested. The performance of the different interpolation methods depends heavily on the interpolated function. Our goal is to select a method, which can be reliably applied to the *cumulative* distributions of deaths observed in Denmark in the 19th century.

The methods of interpolation and separation employed by actuaries and demographers are discussed in Shryock et al. (1993). They give an account of the most frequently used methods of oscillatory interpolation, such as Karup-King's Third-Difference Formula, Sprague's Fifth-Difference Formula, and Beers's Six-Term Ordinary Formula, all of which have been used for years to deal with such problems. All these methods are rooted in the polynomial interpolation. They differ only in the number of knots on the interval, boundary constraints and the degree of the interpolating polynomial.

Another appealing method of polynomial interpolation stems from the modern developments in numeric analysis, which led to the emergence of spline interpolation techniques. Dierckx (1993) provides a systematic introduction to spline theory and discusses the methods of efficient manipulations and numerically stable computations of spline functions. As discussed by Dierckx, any spline can be expressed as a linear combination of b-splines. Therefore the problem of finding an interpolating spline is equivalent to the problem of finding the b-spline coefficients. Once the coefficients have been computed, the interpolated values are easily evaluated by means of the linear combination of b-splines. It is also worth noting that the derivatives and integrals of spline functions can be also calculated in an efficient manner. Application of spline functions to demographic problems can be found in McNeil et al. (1972).

In order to test these methods, the death counts with known single-year-of-age distribution of deaths were aggregated into five-year age groups and then interpolated back into the groups by single year of age. Before carrying out this test, the Lexis map of the distribution deviations was computed for the years 1835–1995, to select the period with roughly the same distribution of the grouped death counts as in the years 1835–1915. The visual analysis shows that the deviations lie within 50% for years prior to 1940, except for the years surrounding the influenza epidemic of 1918. The death distribution in the period starting with the year 1940 is quite different from those observed in the nineteenth century because of rapid mortality changes in the immediately preceding decades. In the end, the years 1916 and 1921–1940 for which single-year-of-age distribution of deaths are available, were selected for testing the interpolation methods.

The interpolation procedures were applied to the *cumulative* death distribution starting at age 5 and ending at age 100, with data points available every five years. The high-order derivatives for the spline function at the boundaries were set to zero, thus providing for a natural spline interpolation procedure. Once the interpolated data have been computed, the deviation of the interpolated death distributions from the original distributions was assessed by several methods (Appendix Table 4).

In the last age group (95–100), all the methods produced negative values for some of the ages because of a rapid function change in this age interval. Trying to circumvent this problem, different boundary conditions were imposed to the spline functions at age 100. Generally, negative interpolated values can be averted by selection custom boundary conditions for spline interpolation. Nevertheless, the death distribution within this group still exhibited an implausible pattern when compared with the original distribution. Thus, results of interpolation for this age group were unsatisfactory when using any of the methods. Testing another interpolation method, e.g. parametric mortality models or developing an algorithm for selection of proper boundary conditions, may be possible solutions to cope with this problem.

In present work, the separation of deaths in this age group has been achieved by applying average death distribution in the period 1921–1940. I have analyzed the trends in death distribution in this age group over time with the linear regression model and it turned out that the trends in proportions over time of deaths were not significant at any age. This justifies the application of the average death distribution (Table 2.1) for separation of deaths in this age group by single year of age.

Table 2.1 The death distribution within the age group 95–99 and in the year 1916 and 1921–1940[2]

AGE	95	96	97	98	99
Males	0.401815	0.267665	0.170289	0.104261	0.055970
Females	0.382720	0.259440	0.114684	0.114684	0.071235

---

[2] The years 1917–1919 were excluded because of abnormal mortality conditions.

Selection of a proper interpolation method for lower age groups follows immediately from the Appendix Table 4. The bold-faced values in each row of this table show the minimal deviation among all interpolation schemes. It is evident from the table that the cubic spline interpolation performs remarkably well, compared to other methods. Consequently this method was applied for interpolation of the real data.

Age zero

Death statistics for the first year of life are too detailed for what is required by this database. Starting with the year 1855, for example, the deaths are recorded by the following intervals: 0–1 month, 1–2, 2–3, 3–6, 6–9 and 9–12 months. Using these data, the deaths in the Lexis triangles at age zero can be computed more accurately than for all other ages.

Let x_u be the upper limit of the age interval and x_l the lower limit. Assuming that the deaths are distributed evenly in the interval $[x_l, x_u]$, the proportions of deaths occurring in the older and younger cohort will be $\pi_1 = (x_u + x_l)/2$ and $\pi_2 = 1 - \pi_1$ respectively. Applying these equations for all age intervals and summing up the deaths, we obtain the death counts by cohort for the first year of life.

In the period from 1835 to 1854, such detailed statistics were not available. In this case, the average distribution of deaths observed in the years 1855–1879 was used to split the death counts by cohorts.

Note that the data for the first year of life were aggregated, instead of separating the death counts by single age and cohort (as was done for all other ages). Thus some information has been lost, and one should be aware of the fact that the database is not planned for use in studies of infant mortality, where the more detailed data can be exploited. Still, the mortality at age zero is necessary for the computation of aggregated demographic characteristics summarizing the experience of the whole age range, e.g. life expectancy at birth.

Ages 100+

In the period 1835–1854, deaths at ages 100 and above were published by the following age groups: 100–105, 105–110 and 110+. From 1855 to 1942, they are given as a single age group 100+. To separate, for example, the age group 100+ one needs to make an assumption about mortality at such advanced ages, because the direct computation of mortality estimates is not possible – not even using the data from other countries. It is evident from Table 2.2, that the absolute death count numbers are very small and the use of complicated separation procedures would hardly influence the mortality estimates at lower ages.

Bearing that in mind, the deaths were separated with the help of exponential distribution[3], which implies that death rates are constant at ages after 100, with the level of mortality described by a single parameter λ. The parameter λ was estimated by fitting this model to the period life table for 1950–1970. For the male population, the estimate of λ was 0.7783 and for females, it was 0.6653.

Table 2.2 The number of deaths above age 100

	PERIOD						
	1835–39	1840–49	1850–59	1860–69	1870–79	1880–89	1890–99
Males	7	19	13	4	7	3	8
Females	16	26	27	15	25	22	25
	1900–09	1910–19	1920–29	1930–42			
Males	6	9	20	35			
Females	40	32	36	68			

Distribution of deaths by Lexis triangles

For the years prior to 1920 the death counts by single age must be separated between the cohorts contributing the deaths into the two Lexis triangles. I used the simplest approach here: the deaths were divided evenly between the cohorts. This assumption is not normally justified, especially for older ages[4] where the mortality rates are particularly high. This must be discussed in more detail, as it is directly related to the mortality estimates.

It is clear that the proportion of deaths in the triangle BCD to the deaths in the rectangle ABCD (Fig. 2.1) depends on the current population structure and the current death rate – and neither is available until the database is completed. A promising approach would be to:

a) estimate the current death rate and the population structure assuming the uniform distribution of deaths in the Lexis rectangle;
b) develop a statistical model which takes into account the dependence of the distribution on age and year;
c) estimate the model and use the predictions from this model to redistribute the deaths between cohorts;
d) re-estimate the current population and death rate using redistributed death counts, and then repeat steps c) and d) until convergence is reached.

---

[3] Death counts for the years 1835–1854 were aggregated into the single 100+ age group before the separation.

[4] The differences are highest at age zero but in this case more detailed statistics are available for the estimation of separation factors.

Another approach would be to develop a linear model for the proportion of deaths in one of the two Lexis triangles and estimate it using existing data collected on the cohort basis. The predictions of this model can be used later to separate deaths by cohort. This approach has been used, for example, by Condran et al. (1991) and by Wilmoth in his work on Swedish data[5]. Wilmoth also presented seven linear models useful in the analysis of the proportion of deaths in the Lexis triangles.

This approach is however complicated by the fact that we actually need to build a backward projection, since there are no detailed data available for the 19th century. Wilmoth used Swedish deaths for the years 1901–1991 to estimate the model and then he derived the predicted proportions of lower triangle deaths for the years 1751–1900 based on the model predictions in the year 1910, with the corrections for birth counts. It is still not clear if the model predictions for the 19th century are reliable, because mortality regimes and population structures of Sweden in the 19th and 20th centuries are quite different.

In the present work on construction of the Danish mortality database, neither or these two procedures had been applied to the Danish data. The data on deaths in Denmark are available by cohort from 1921 and onwards, and by five-year age groups for 1835–1915. The use of the advanced methods to separate death counts by cohort hardly improves the overall quality of mortality estimates for the period prior 1921 at all, since for most of the years, the single-year-of-age death counts are already interpolated from the original deaths given in five-year age groups. Application of either of these two methods would be of little practical importance for the construction of the Danish mortality database. For this reason, I split the death counts evenly between the cohorts and made no attempts to estimate the separation factors.

2.5.2 Population

1976–2000

The population counts for these years have been published as estimates for January 1st and for all ages by single year of age. I have included these population counts in the database without any modifications, with the exception of the cohorts for which I computed the estimates by the extinct cohort method (see below).

Population estimates for this period, stem from the Central Personal Register, which was established in 1968. Since that time every resident of Denmark has a CPR number and the information about him is stored in the databases of Danmarks

---

[5] See the online documentation at http://demog.berkeley.edu/wilmoth/mortality/

Statistik. Based on this information, Danmarks Statistik has been publishing annual estimates of the Danish population since 1976.

1906–1975

The population estimates for these years were obtained directly from Danmarks Statistik by Ulla Larsen. The population is that of January 1st, and it is given by single year of age. The estimates are based on the information available from the census questionnaires along with additional non-published data. More specific information about the source of these data and the procedures used to produce the estimates is not available. At advanced ages, the population counts were aggregated into a single age group: 85+ for the years 1906–1940, 100+ for the years 1941–1970, and 99+ for 1971–1975. These age groups do not pose significant problems, since the population at these ages can be computed by the extinct cohort method.

1870–1901

Population by single age is available for this period from censuses held in 1870, 1880, 1890 and 1901 (see also Appendix Table 2).

The first problem is that the censuses were carried out on February 1st rather than on January 1st as required by the database. Therefore, one needs to correct the census population by taking into account the population trends over time. To make the adjustment, a simple regression model $\ln \tilde{N}_y = \beta_0 + \beta_1 y$ was fitted separately to each age x, with $\tilde{N}_y$ being the population at January 1st in the year y (1870.085[6], 1890.085, ... 1906, 1907, ... 1917) (Fig. 2.1). All population time series used to fit the data, stop just before the influenza epidemic and include only cohorts with a loglinear increase in birth counts[7]. This restriction seems to be reasonable because the series of $\tilde{N}_y$ are highly correlated with the birth count of the corresponding cohort and because the number of births fell markedly in 1910 for both males and females. This drop in the number of births highly affects the population structure and can worsen both the fit of regression and the adjustment we now must make.

Finally, the population estimates for January 1st were calculated by linear interpolation of the census population using the age-specific derivatives predicted by the regression for January 1st.

Another problem that needed to be addressed was the estimation of population between censuses. I did this in a standard way by using the natural balance equation

---

[6] The fractional part of these numbers reflects the fact that the censuses were taken on February 1st.

[7] For males cohorts 1835–1909 were used for estimation of the model and the goodness of fit was $R^2=0.981$. For females the cohorts were 1835–1908 and $R^2=0.980$.

(an alternative name for this procedure is "intercensal cohort survival method", cf. e.g. Wilmoth, BMD documentation[5]). The population $\tilde{N}_{x,y}$ aged x at the time of first census y will be aged $x+\Delta$ at the time of second census $y+\Delta$, where Δ is the time between censuses. We know the values $\tilde{N}_{x,y}$, $\tilde{N}_{x+\Delta,y+\Delta}$ from the censuses and we know the number of deaths $D_{z,\Delta}$ in the cohort $z = y-x-1$ attending age x in the year y during period Δ from death statistics. Given these numbers, we are able to compute the inconsistency error between them for a single cohort:

$$\delta_{x,y} = \tilde{N}_{x,y} - D_{z,\Delta} - \tilde{N}_{x+\Delta,y+\Delta} \qquad (2.1)$$

In the ideal case, i.e. if the population is closed for migration and no errors exist in population and death statistics, the inconsistency error δ is zero. In real populations it can deviate significantly from zero, because of migration or inaccuracies in the census population which can be produced, for example, by different coverage in two censuses; or by errors in the recorded age at death in the period between censuses.

In application to Danish data, the error δ was distributed evenly among the Lexis triangles of the cohort z in the period from y to $y+\Delta$. If independent estimates of migration would be available, more elaborated procedures for distribution of the error δ can be devised, but the estimates of migration for a given period are not available for Denmark.

Sometimes this method produces negative population numbers in the period between censuses. Such unacceptable results are mainly due to the following three sources of errors:

a) errors in the census population estimates and death registration;
b) errors introduced by the interpolation procedure;
c) invalid assumption of even distribution of the error δ among Lexis triangles (this is closely related to the age- and time-specific patterns of migration);
d) different population coverage in two subsequent censuses.

The problem was not explored more deeply as the negative numbers occurred only at very high ages where population can be estimated by the extinct cohort method.

It is worth noting that the error δ is particularly high in this period because of high emigration from Denmark, mostly to America (Hvidt, 1971). The total migration numbers, which can be computed from the database, appeared to be consistent with those given in Matthiessen (1970).

1834–1869

Population statistics for this period are also available from censuses, but population numbers are given only by five-year age groups (Appendix Table 2). Before employing the natural balance equation method, we need to estimate the single-age population structure. I rigorously tested two methods before applying the superior one to the real data.

The first method is a combination of the natural balance equation method and the extinct cohort method. In this method, some known *single-age* population is projected back to the time of the previous census using the death counts in the intercensual period. Any migration that may have occurred in this period is not taken into account. As a result we obtain population estimates by single age at the time of previous census. The resulting population estimates are used to compute population distribution at the time of the previous census and then to prorate official census estimates by single year of age.

Let $\tilde{N}_{x,y}$ be the population aged x at the beginning of year y and in the cohort $z = y - x - 1$. Then the population at the time of previous census is

$$\tilde{N}_{x-\Delta, y-\Delta} = \tilde{N}_{x,y} + D_{z,\Delta} \tag{2.2}$$

where Δ is the time between censuses and $D_{z,\Delta}$ is the number of deaths in the cohort z during period Δ. Using the estimated single-age population distribution at the time of the previous census $y-\Delta$ $\pi_{x,y-\Delta} = \dfrac{\tilde{N}_{x,y-\Delta}}{\sum_x \tilde{N}_{x,y-\Delta}}$ it is easy to separate the available census data by single year of age.

The second method is the interpolation of the *cumulative* population distribution by the natural cubic spline. This involves the computation of b-spline coefficients and the evaluation of interpolating spline by single year of age. The procedure is essentially the same as that applied to the separation of deaths aggregated by 5-year age groups.

Both methods have been tested on population data for the period 1925–1974. Single-year-of-age population estimates available for this period have been aggregated into age groups of 1834, 1840 and 1860 censuses and then redistributed back by single year of age by spline interpolation and the natural balance equation methods. I applied the method of the natural balance equation with step Δ equal to 10 years. That is, the population in the year 1925 was reconstructed using the single-year-of-age population of 1935. The population in the year 1926 was reconstructed using the population of 1936, et cetera. Subsequently, I computed the aggregated index of relative deviation $\delta = \sum_x \frac{(\tilde{N}_x - \hat{N}_x)^2}{\tilde{N}_x}$ between the original and the reconstructed populations and plotted it for each year from 1925 to 1974 in Fig. 2.2. The quantity $\tilde{N}_x$ is the original population and $\hat{N}_x$ is the redistributed population. Note also, that the method of natural balance equation produces the same single-year-of-age population estimates, regardless of the level of aggregation of the original data while the outcome of the spline interpolation procedure depends on which age groups were used for aggregating the original population estimates.

It is apparent from Fig. 2.2, that the method of the natural balance equation with a small number of exceptions, reproduces the original population more accurately than the spline interpolation procedure, especially if the population is given in the broader age groups, as in the 1834 census.

Therefore, I estimated the single-age distribution of population for this period by means of the combination of natural balance equation and extinct cohort method. The gaps between censuses were filled in using the same procedure as in the period from 1870 to 1901.

Extinct cohort population

Population estimates at advanced ages pose an additional problem. As shown in the Appendix Table 2.2 they are not available up to the highest ages at death as required by the database. Thus we need to estimate missing population or redistribute available population groups, i.e. 85+. Another concern is the quality of population estimates at such advanced ages. A commonly recognized problem is age misreporting in censuses, which becomes more severe as we advance to higher ages and into earlier years.

Taking into account all these considerations, population at the highest ages has been estimated by the extinct cohort method (Vincent, 1951). This method is widely recognized as producing reliable population estimates at older ages, where migration can be safely ignored. The extinct cohort population estimates were computed for all ages above 80. The last cohort with extinct population was 1887 for males and 1883 for females.

For Denmark, however, the procedure is more complicated than the standard method because the coverage of Danish statistics was changed in 1920. In this year, South Jutland (Sønderjylland) became a part of Denmark, increasing the population of the country by about 163,000 people or 5.5%. The population of South Jutland was enumerated as a stand-alone geographical area in the 1921 census and death counts were included in the official statistics starting with the year 1921. Producing

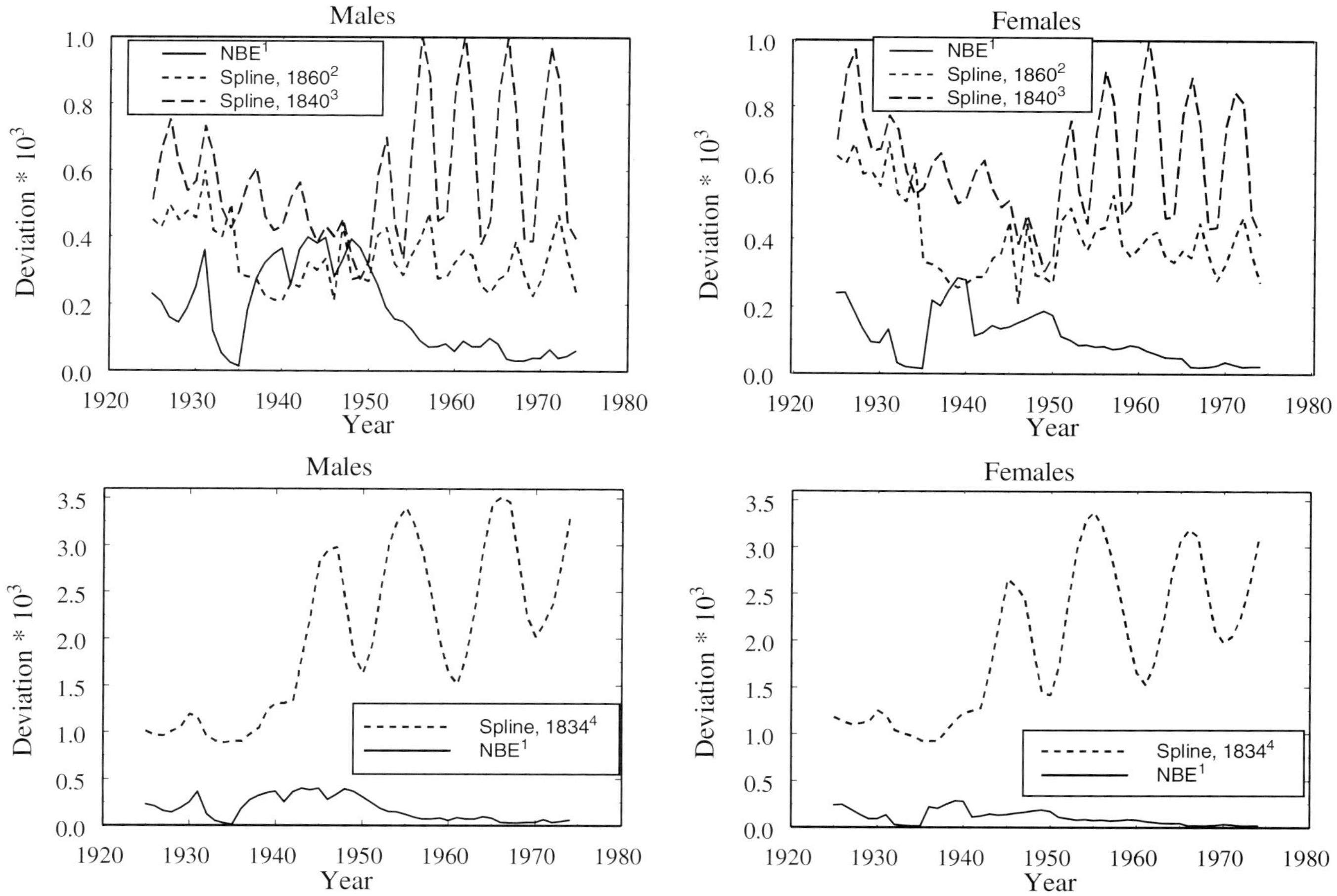

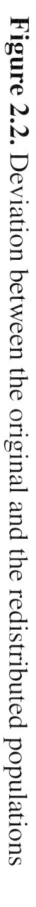

Figure 2.2. Deviation between the original and the redistributed populations

[1] The method of the natural balance equation.
[2] The spline interpolation of the population distribution of 1860 census.
[3] The spline interpolation of the population distribution of 1840 census.
[4] The spline interpolation of the population distribution of 1834 census.

extinct cohort population estimates for years prior to 1921, requires that the deaths that occurred in this part of Denmark be excluded from the computations. The fraction of total deaths that has to be excluded was taken to be equal to the population of South Jutland on January 1st 1921. This population was published by single year of age in the 1921 census.

Population at exact age

The calculation of population at risk N_x (Fig. 2.1, line BC) is based on the assumption of even migration distribution:

$$N_{x,y} = \frac{1}{2}\left((\tilde{N}_{x-1,y} - {}^2D_{x-1,y}) + (\tilde{N}_{x,y+1} + {}^1D_{x,y})\right) \quad (2.3)$$

where $\tilde{N}_{x,y}$, ${}^1D_{x,y}$, ${}^2D_{x,y}$ are the population estimates at January 1st, death counts in timing one and two, and in the year y and at age x, respectively.

These population estimates are particularly useful for computing both the period and the cohort life tables constructed by the cohort method and for fitting mortality models.

3. A descriptive analysis of the evolution of the Danish population with focus on mortality

3.1 Danish population changes over the period 1835–2000

Data on the total Danish population by sex and year are shown in Fig. 3.1. In the period from 1835 to 2000, the male population increased from 605,300 to 2,634,100 and the female population from 619,000 to 2,695,900, which corresponds to an annual rate of increase of 0.97%, or approximately 25,000 people per year. Females outnumbered males for the whole period of observation and especially in the last two decades. This can be explained by the highest gap ever between male and female mortality observed in this last period. The persistent growth of the Danish population continued until 1981, when the total population started to decline. This decline lasted until 1985, when the population began to grow again. The population leap in 1920, resulting from the reunification of Denmark and South Jutland is also clearly visible on the graph. The population of South Jutland at that time constituted about 5.5% of the total population of Denmark.

Declining mortality and fertility, two attributes of the demographic transition, had a profound influence on the age structure of the Danish population. Fig. 3.2 shows the striking differences between 1835–1840 and 1995–2000 age structures. The first is characterized by a high proportion of children and young people, while proportions of the oldest old (80+) are negligible. In contrast, the contemporary age structure of the population exhibits substantially reduced proportions of young people and dramatically increased proportions of the oldest-old. In the male population the proportion of children aged 0–10 dropped 45%, while the proportion of males aged 80 quadrupled and that of 90-year-olds rose by a factor of eight. The changes in the female age structure are even more impressive, the proportion of 90-year-olds in the period 1995–2000, for example, is 14 times higher than in 1835–1840.

Comparing age structure of the Danish population at the beginning and at the end of an observation period helps us to pick up a general pattern of changes in the age structure: reductions in the number of children and increases in the population of elderly. This is well known from demographic research and publications of national statistical offices. Less known is time-specific changes in age structure. Such analysis, however, requires presentation of significantly larger amounts of information. One way to tackle this problem is to employ the Lexis map techniques, which is widely used in demographic research (e.g. Vaupel et al., 1998).

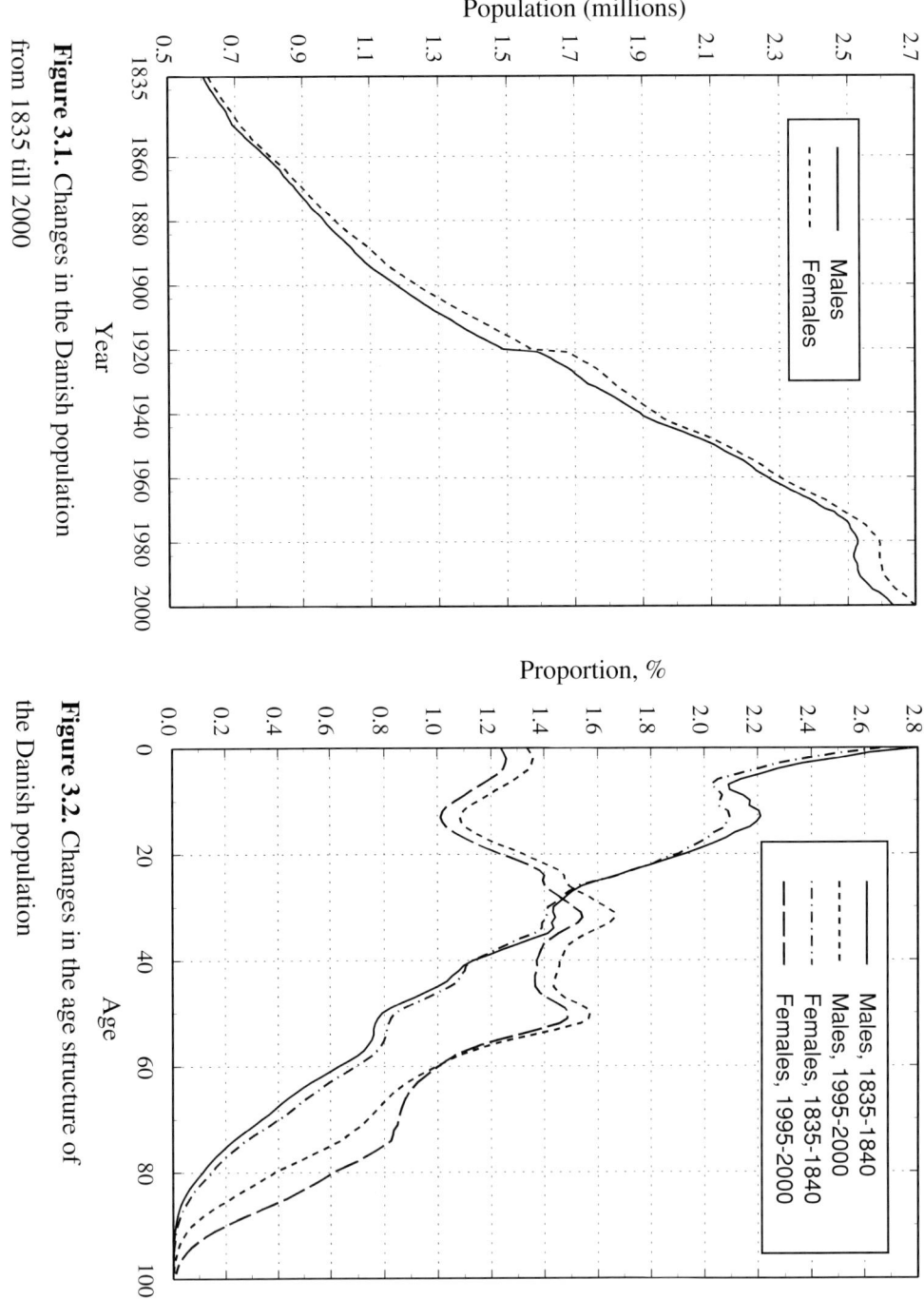

Figure 3.1. Changes in the Danish population from 1835 till 2000

Figure 3.2. Changes in the age structure of the Danish population

Fig. 3.3 presents the Lexis maps of Danish population distribution plotted over age and time. The Danish population distribution is plotted separately for males and females. Each small rectangle on these maps refers to a proportion (%) of the population on January 1st at a certain age of the total population in the current year. In other words Fig. 3.3 shows simultaneously 166 population distributions: one distribution for one year from 1835 to 2000. Each distribution includes 100 values for each age-specific proportion of a population in the current year (one value for single age: 0 ... 98, 99+). The scale on the right partitions all population proportions into several groups and the proportions included in one group are assigned the same color and pattern. For example, all proportions which are higher than 2% are plotted in black as indicated by the highest rectangle on the scale legend.

The contour maps (Fig. 3.3) permit us to see all the population proportions at a glance. The contour lines themselves, help us to follow the development of the Danish age structure over time. If we look, for example, at contour line 2.00, we observe that it remained almost constant at the age about 10 and then it suddenly dropped to zero in 1920. This contour line circumscribes ages and years with the highest density observed in the Danish population, i.e. childhood ages in the 19th century. They appear as a black area in Fig. 3.3. In the beginning of the 1920s, this area virtually disappears and it comes into view again only in the late 1940s, but now as several diagonal lines. Emergence of this area in the late 1940s is attributed to the very high fertility in the post-war period, generally referred to in demographic literature as the baby boom.

Other contour lines help us to follow the evolution of Danish age distribution at other ages. In the female population, for example, contour line 0.33 starts at age 71 in 1835 and moves to age 87 in 2000. This means that the population proportions at these ages are nearly the same. If we look at age 70 itself, the proportion of the female population at this age in the period 1835–1860 were about 0.36% (slightly higher than the contour line 0.33). In the 1990s, age 70 belongs to a different area on a Lexis map $(0.66–1.00)^8$ and the proportion of population is equal to 0.8%: a two-fold increase.

Growth of contour lines over time designates increase in the population proportions over time. If we look again at the contour line 0.33 in the female population, after being relatively stable until 1940, it shows a sudden upturn (clearly visible on the map). This marks onset of rapid population aging in Denmark, which continues until present time.

Another way to look at Danish population aging is by comparing the observed

---

[8] Hereafter I will use (5-10) notation to denote areas on a Lexis map, which lie between contour lines equal to 5 and 10.

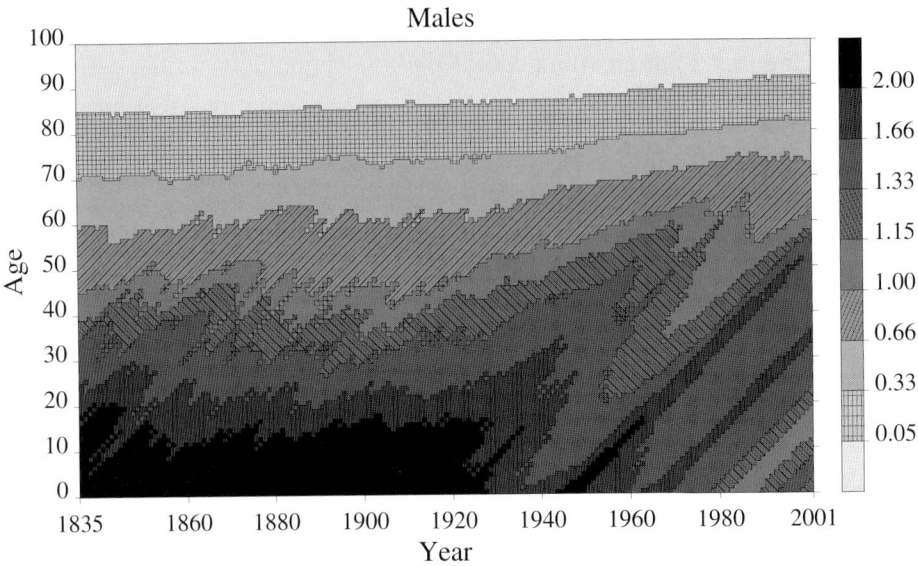

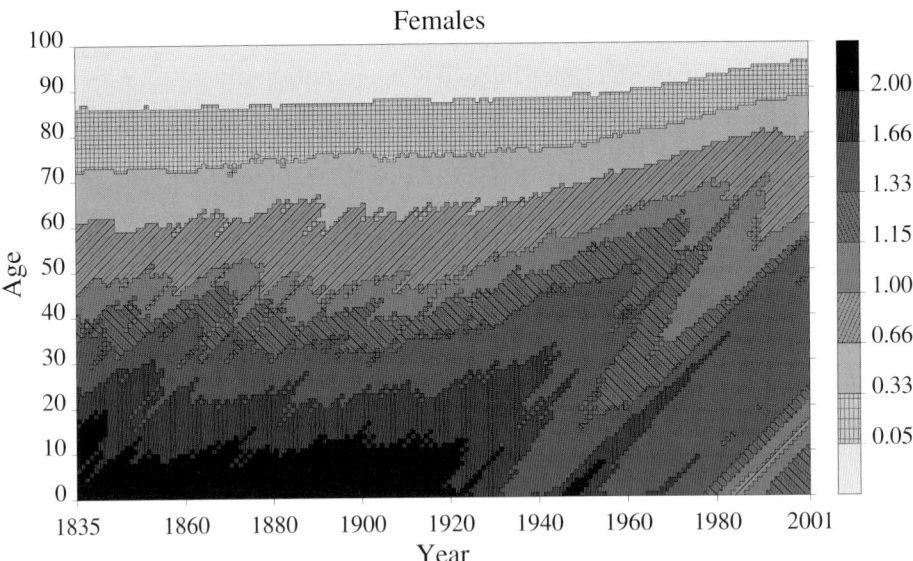

Figure 3.3. Danish population distribution (%)

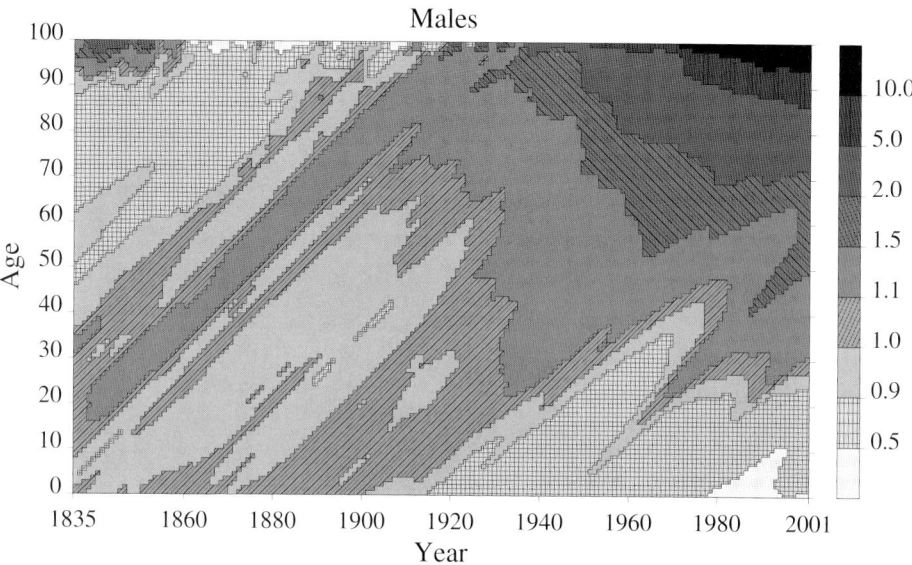

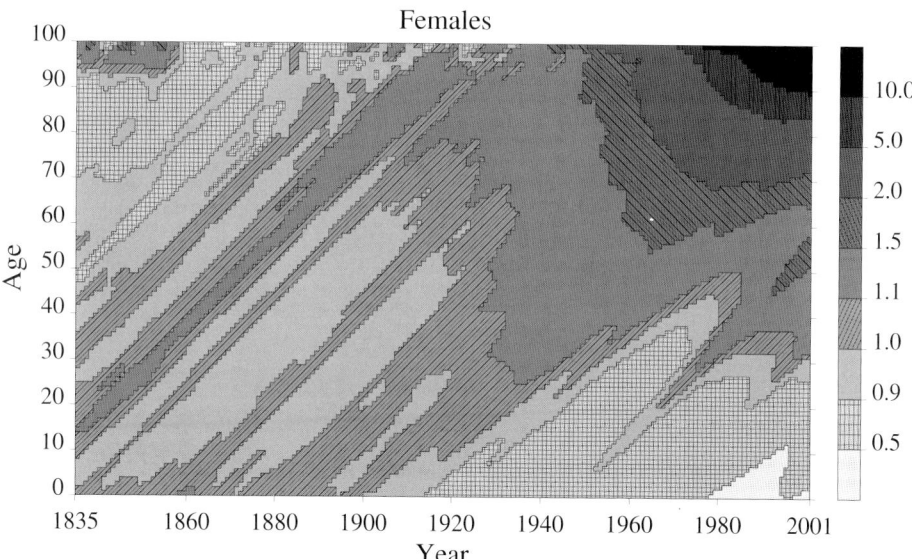

Smoothed with 3x3 bivariate Epanechnikov kernel.

Figure 3.4. Ratio of the Danish population distribution to the average levels in 1835-1920

values to some standard age distribution. As it is seen from Fig. 3.3, a rapid transition in the Danish population structure occurred in the 1920s. Before that time, the structure of the Danish population was more or less stable. Therefore, I decide to divide the matrix of the population proportions shown in Fig. 3.3 by the average population distribution over period 1835–1920. To enhance the presentation, the resulting surface (Fig. 3.4) has been smoothed on a 3x3 matrix with Epanechnikov weights (Appendix 5).

Fig 3.4 emphasizes dramatic changes in the Danish population distribution since the 1920s. An especially marked increase is visible in the proportions of the oldest-old; these emerging areas are colored in dark gray and black in Fig. 3.4. The areas (5–10) and (>10.0) correspond to the ages where proportions are 5 and 10 times greater than in 1835–1920. The increase in the proportions of oldest-old has been accompanied by corresponding reductions in proportions of ages below 30 (by a factor about 1.5–2). This phenomenon is portrayed by the areas (0.5–0.9) and (<0.5) - the areas where the proportions are lower than in 1835–1920.

Analysis of changes in Danish population distributions ultimately point to the fact that the growth of the population of elderly was strikingly higher than at other ages. As follows from Fig. 3.1, the total population of Denmark has increased by a factor of 4.35 since 1835. We would expect that the population gains differ considerably among the ages and deviation from this average rate of increase is high among the ages. Fig 3.5 provides quantitative information regarding such differences.

For any year y and age x population aged $[x,x+1)$ $\tilde{N}_{x,y}$ at the beginning of the year y (Fig. 2.1) can be represented as

$$\tilde{N}_{x,y} = \tilde{N}_{x,1835} \exp\left[\int_{1835}^{y} r_x(u)du\right]$$

where $r_x(y)$ is the instantaneous rate of population growth in given year y and age x. Surface of $r_x(y)$ can be estimated from the observed population levels. Quantity $\exp\left[\int_{1835}^{y} r_x(u)du\right]$ can in its turn be estimated for any year y and age x from the surface of $r_x(y)$ (this can be interpreted as an age-specific population growth factor since 1835). This quantity is shown in Fig. 3.5, indicating for each year relative gains in the single-year-of-age population groups. Note that this is not the same as the ratio of the observed population at age x in the year y to the population at the same age x in the year 1835, because the population observed in the intermediate years are also included in the computations of the instantaneous growth rates.

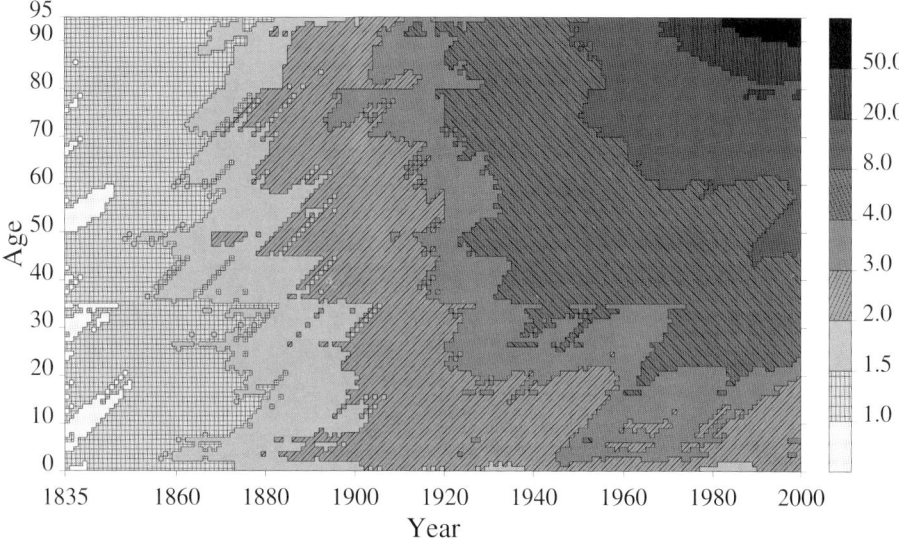

Estimates are based on the surface of instantaneous growth rate rather than on on dividing of the current population by the population in 1835.

Figure 3.5. Cumulative growth rate of the Danish population

Until 1870, the population at each age group increased more or less uniformly by a factor of 1.5. This is depicted by almost a vertical contour line (1.5). Until 1920, such a pattern of age-specific increase continued to prevail in the Danish population, except for the relative gains at older ages which were slightly higher than at young ages. At ages above 60, the population until 1920, increased by a factor of approximately 3–3.5, while at ages younger than 30 by 2.3–2.7.

Starting with the 1920s, rapid growth of the elderly population considerably outnumbered population gains at younger ages. Already in the 1950s, the population aged 70 and over were 8 times higher than at the beginning of the observation period (contour line 8), while population aged <30 increased only by factor about 3.5. Further exploration shows even more striking gains at old ages (areas (8–20), (20–50), (>50)). At the beginning of the year 2000, population in age group 60–70 rose approximately by factor of 10, at ages 70–80 by 15, at ages 80–90 by 35 and by a factor of more than 50 for the ages over 90. For a comparison, at ages less than 20, the relative gains are only 2.5–3 (area (2–3)).

Summarizing our results on the analysis of the Danish population changes over the period of 1835–2000, I would like to emphasize several of perhaps the most important findings. First, the total population of Denmark continuously grew from

1835 until 1980, but the growth sharply decelerated in the 1970s and the population began to even decline for several years in the 1980s. In the last few years, the growth of total population has begun to resume again. Second, the analysis of the age structure of the Danish population shows that it was relatively stable until 1920. Afterwards, its shape changed considerably, characterized now by the increased proportions of the elderly population and reduced proportions of the young population. Finally, over time, the Danish population increased approximately by a factor of 4.35 (from 1.22 million people in 1835 to 5.33 in 2000) and in the recent decades, the growth was driven mostly by increasing proportion of the elderly where relative gains were strikingly high.

3.2 The Danish mortality evolution

3.2.1 Life expectancy at birth

Mortality and fertility are two major driving forces beyond the evolution of any population. In this section, I focus on the developments in Danish mortality over time. We begin with an analysis of the changes in Danish life expectancy at birth. This demographic indicator conventionally summarizes the changes in the mortality regime as an overall measure of mortality. To follow the changes in life expectancy, I computed the single-year period life tables and plotted the life expectancy at birth in Fig. 3.6.

As indicated by this figure, Danish life expectancy has undergone remarkable changes since the middle of the nineteenth century. In the year 1835, males lived an average of 40 years and females 42 years. By 1999, these figures had risen to 74 and 79 years of age, respectively.

Until the 1870s, the gains in life expectancy were negligible both for males and females. Fitting a simple linear regression model[9]

$$e_0(y) = \beta_0 + \beta_1 y \tag{3.1}$$

to the trends in the life expectancy gives 0.049 for males and 0.033 for females (Table 3.1). Curves are jagged due to the frequent epidemics of infectious diseases, which plagued the country at the time. Consequently, the standard error is high and the estimates are not statistically significant.

The decade 1870–80 marks an onset of persistent increase in life expectancy at birth. The increase was rather moderate before 1900, but accelerated afterwards. Until the year 1950, this increase was quite strong, with an annual gain of 0.318 for males and 0.315 for females. Starting in the 1950s life expectancy improvement

---

[9] $e_0(y)$ - life expectancy at birth, y - calendar year.

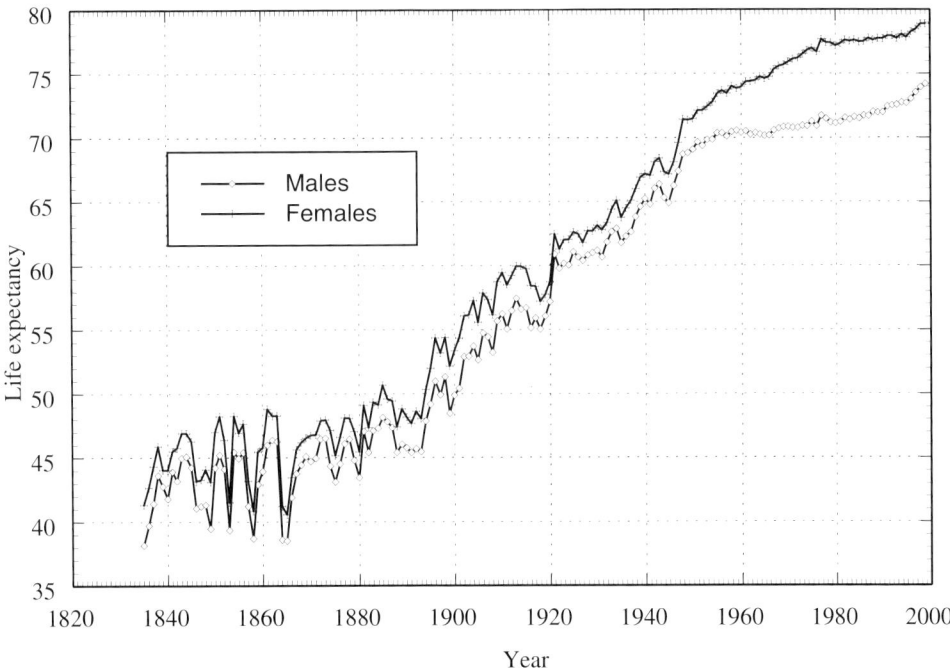

Figure 3.6. Danish life expectancy at birth

significantly decelerated, especially for males. Until 1980, male life expectancy gains were close to zero, while female life expectancy still continued to grow, but on a slower pace. The year 1980 is another turning point in Fig. 3.6. In this year, the male life expectancy started to grow faster than before, while the female curve almost stagnated. Such development persisted until the mid-1990s, when the life expectancy growth considerably accelerated, now both for males and females. Even the estimates given in Table 3.1 for the last period are based only on four points, they

Table 3.1 Annual gains in Danish life expectancy in the selected periods (This table includes the estimates of the slope of the model (3.1).

Period	Males	Females
1835–1869	0.049 (0.041)	0.033 (0.040)
1870–1949	0.318 (0.007)	0.315 (0.007)
1950–1979	0.060 (0.006)	0.192 (0.005)
1980–1995	0.108 (0.007)	0.042 (0.007)
1996–1999	0.382 (0.038)	0.232 (0.055)

give an impression in development of Danish life expectancy in the most recent years. We can see that the male life expectancy gains were the highest over all periods and that the female gains were also quite strong.

The difference between male and female life expectancy can also be clearly followed in Fig. 3.6. For the whole period of observation, female life expectancy was always higher than that of the male. In the period from 1835–1950, there are no systematic changes: the male–female difference is irregular, hovering between one and four years. Due to different progress made in life expectancy between sexes, a large gap between male and female life expectancy began to manifest itself starting with the 1950s. This gap reached its peak in 1980, when females outlived males on average by more than 6 years. Starting with 1980, the remarkable decline in life expectancy difference between sexes took place. The convergence of male and female life expectancy continued until the most recent years and the difference in 1999–2000 was about 4.7 years.

3.2.2 Period survivorship

The analysis of life expectancy evolution helps us to highlight the most prominent changes in mortality regime over time, but age specific differences in survival are left behind the scene. Later in this chapter, the emphasis is laid on the age specific developments in Danish mortality, which will be presented from different angles.

I start with the exploration of period survival (Fig. 3.7). I have extracted survivorship from a set of period life tables computed by the single calendar year and plotted it in a form of a Lexis map in Fig. 3.7. Each survival function includes estimates of a proportion of people surviving to a certain age in a given calendar year.

Years 1835–1890 are characterized by high infant mortality. If we look at contour line 80, it stays almost at a constant level over this period for both males and females. The average age for males is about 3 years and for females is about 4 (for females it is slightly higher because of lower infant mortality). Only 80% of the boys and girls survived to respective ages during this period. Until 1950, this contour line rose remarkably up to the age 61 in the male population and to the age 68 in the female. In the following years, this contour line reached age 65 for males and 70 for females. In other words, about 80% of the contemporary population survive to the age of 65 among males and to the age of 70 among females. The difference between figures for the 19th century - 3 and 4 years respectively - is striking.

Similar impressive progress in the reduction of the death rates can be followed by the contour lines 95 and 90. These lines appeared on the Lexis map only in the first half of the 20th century, reaching by the end of century, 46 and 57 years of age for males, and 53 and 62 for females. In other words, 95% of males now survive to the age 46 and 90% to the age 57. For females, consequently, 95% of population survive to the age of 53 and 90% to the age of 62.

Improvements in survival at other ages were also remarkable. Over the period 1835–1880, only half of the males and females survived to the age 50, but at the end of 20th century, 50% of males were living to the age 77 and 50% of females to the age 82. At oldest-old ages, notable gains in survival are to be observed as well. During the years 1835–1860, the proportion of males survived to the age 90 was about 0.7% and the proportion of females was about 1.5%. In the year 2000, these figures are 9% and 20%, respectively.

3.2.3 Mortality

Another way to look at Danish mortality developments over time is to explore the Lexis maps of Danish death rates. In order to grasp the evolution of the entire mortality surface of Denmark, the central death rates have been computed by single year and age, and plotted in Fig. 3.8. The death rate is assumed to be constant over a Lexis rectangle, and it is painted in a single color and pattern on the Lexis maps. The Lexis maps presented in Fig. 3.8 are plotted without any use of interpolation and smoothing techniques, so they reflect the original data underlying the analysis.

As before, the scale shown on the right divides the whole surface into seven areas. Each area on the map corresponds to a certain range of death rates.

For example, the area with the lowest death rates (<0.002) is colored in light gray and appears in Fig. 3.8 only starting with the beginning of the 20th century in the age group 10–15.

The trends in the contour lines allow us to follow the evolution of mortality over time. The contour line itself shows the location of a particular level of mortality over age and time. For example, on the female mortality map, the contour line corresponding to the mortality level of 0.008 starts at age 23 in 1835 and ends at age 59 in 1999. This means that the risk of death for a 23-year-old female in the year 1835 was equal to the risk of death of a 59-year-old female in 1999. This shows an impressive age-specific shift in the mortality level.

Because human mortality increases almost exponentially starting at approximately 30 years of age, the shift of contour lines into the higher ages would portray the progress made in reduction of death rates. The slope of the contour lines reflects the rate of this progress. Childhood mortality reductions can be seen in the shrinkage of the area of very high mortality in the first years of life. Especially striking is the reduction of infant mortality $_1q_0$, which fell from 148 per 1,000 in the 1855–1865 to 8 in 1985–1995 for males and from 124 to 6 for females.

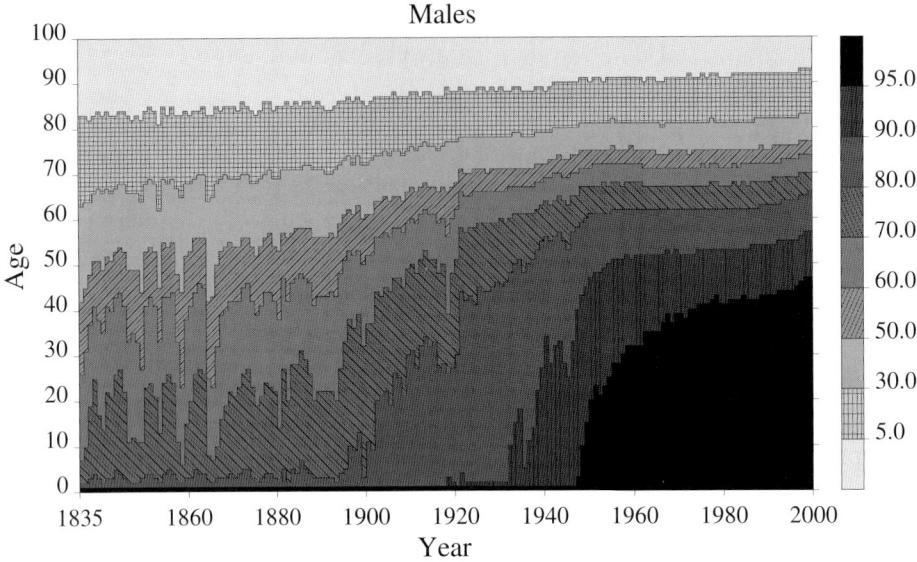
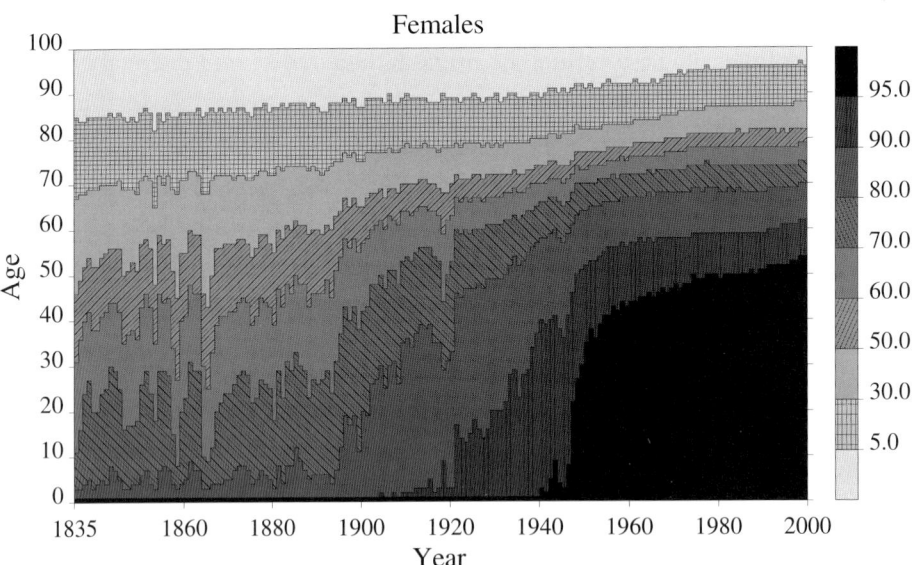

Figure 3.7. Danish survivorship by single calendar year

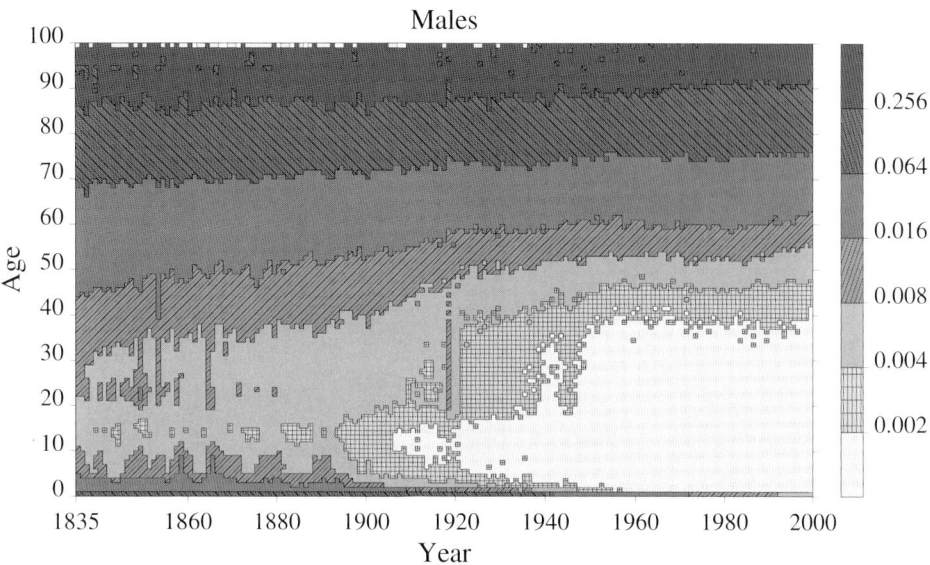
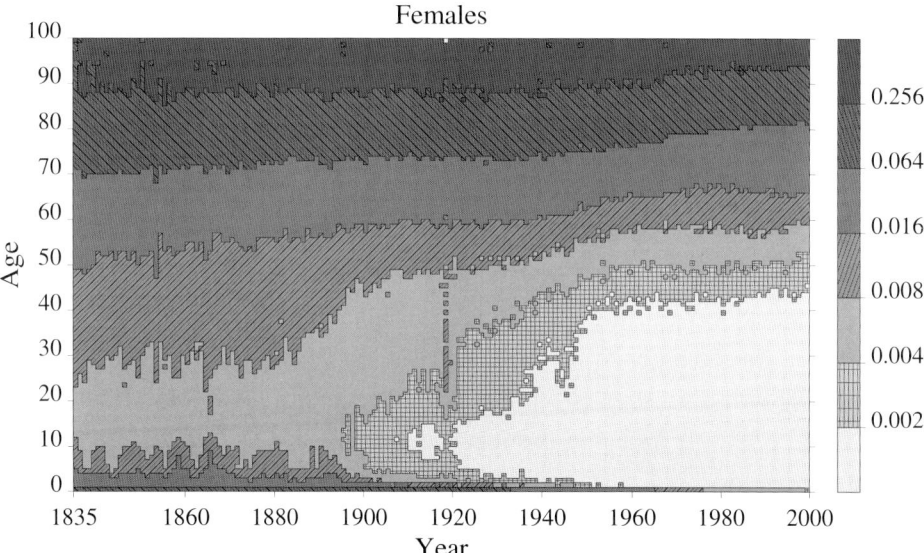

Figure 3.8. Danish death rates

Fig 3.8 permits us to identify the timing of mortality changes and their age-specific features. Over time the Danish mortality decreased generally at all ages, but the progress in reduction of death rates was not uniform over age and time. Moreover it did not follow the same pattern in the male and female populations, especially in the second part of the 20th century.

The onset of the rapid mortality decline occurred in the late 1890s. This is the time during which the areas of the low mortality (<0.002 and 0.002–0.004) began to form. These areas are portrayed in light gray and light gray with rectangle fill in Fig. 3.8 and correspond to mortality levels below 0.4% and 0.2%, respectively. The mortality reductions prior to this period are somewhat less regular except for the ages around 50. The latter generalization should be viewed with caution, however, as the overall quality of mortality estimates in the 19th century is less reliable than in the 20th century. Progress in reduction of death rates at older ages (70+) was very slow and no appreciable gains in mortality reductions can be observed until the 1950s.

Female mortality at young and middle ages (0–60) fell noticeably from the 1890s to the 1950s, while male mortality gains were more moderate. Starting with the 1950s, male mortality stagnated. This is evident in Fig. 3.8, where the contour lines (e.g. 0.008) rose until 1950, but then remained at a constant level or even declined there after. In the 1990s, there were some positive changes in the mortality dynamics as it is indicated by the upward bend in the contour lines, especially in the age group 45–65. For example, the male death rate at age 65 declined from a level of 53 per 1000 in 1835 to 25 in 1945 and then increased to 30 in 1970; until the year 1999 it declined again to a level of 22 per 1000. The stagnation in mortality can be seen on the female map as well, but it occurred later in time. This difference in mortality dynamics between the sexes (earlier stagnation of male death rates) had a major impact at the emergence of the gap between male and female mortality - a matter which we will discuss later on. It is important to note that the infant mortality continued to decline over time and has reached now the lowest level in the history of the Danish population.

Somewhat surprising, is that starting in the 1950s, when reductions in middle-age mortality were low, considerable progress occurred at older ages (70+). Again, male mortality reductions lagged well behind those of females, but the progress in both populations is apparent on the Lexis maps (Fig. 3.8). The gains in the older age groups were not as exceptional as the mortality reductions in childhood and middle ages. Nevertheless, this observation is rather important, because it shows that the elimination of premature deaths at young and middle ages is not the only factor contributing to an increase in Danish life expectancy.

The cohorts that reached 90 in the 1970s, were born in the 1880s - a time when childhood and infant mortality fell dramatically. It might be the case that the progress at advanced ages can be attributed to the improved health conditions in childhood. Additional research is required in order to test this hypothesis.

Another important issue in relation to the reductions in oldest-old mortality is the fact that the quality of statistics improves over time. It has been shown by Preston et al. (1999) that age misreporting (not necessarily age exaggeration) at advanced ages results in lower mortality estimates computed from erroneous data. This means that improvements in oldest-old mortality can be masked by age misreporting, which might be present in the data for earlier periods.

Period effects are also clearly manifested in Fig. 3.8. They can be traced in the long vertical lines of the exceptional mortality. The high ridges of mortality in 1853 and 1918, for example, reflect the aftermath of epidemics of cholera and Spanish influenza. The Second World War appears as an elevated mortality rate at ages 18–35 on both maps, but the excess of mortality is clearly higher for males than for females.

The other strength of the Lexis maps shown in Fig. 3.8, is that they reveal age-specific mortality differences, which might otherwise go unnoticed. Consider the influenza epidemic of 1918 – this is the most dramatic occurrence of the civilized world in the 20th century (with the exception, of course, of the First and Second World Wars). The impact of this epidemic on the overall mortality is clearly visible in Fig. 3.8, although it is almost imperceptible from the trends in crude death rates (figure with trends in crude death rates is not included). The crude death rate in 1918 was 13.2 per 1,000 per annum for males and 12.9 for females, while the average mortality rates in the years 1916, 1917, 1919 and 1920 were 13.4 and 13.0, respectively. The difference between the rates is negligible, which might give an impression that the mortality regimes in 1918 and in adjacent years were similar. The reason for our inability to detect the period effect of the influenza epidemic of 1918 from trends in the crude death rates is that this epidemic was extremely age-selective. The young people (age<40), were the ones who suffered most under this epidemic, while older people were nearly unaffected. If we compute the crude death rates for the same periods, but for ages 20–40 only, the difference is marked: 10.3 versus 5.6 for males and 9.0 versus 5.4 for females.

To complete the presentation of the Danish mortality surface, I would like to provide a more detailed discussion of the factors governing the two most important features of mortality maps: a) the decline in mortality at the end of 19th century and b) the stagnation in mortality in the last decades of the 20th century. I will discuss the first phenomenon only briefly here, since a full examination falls well outside of the scope of this study. The second phenomenon will be explored in more detail later on, as more statistical data are available, which enables us to make the comparisons between countries and to investigate the differences in cause-specific mortality and in social-economic variables.

There is a vast amount of literature devoted to mortality decline in the 19th century and at the beginning of the 20th century, but there has hitherto been no systematic study of the mortality transition in Denmark. The most prominent work in this field is perhaps the monograph of Matthiessen (1970), which focuses on the construction of the total mortality, fertility and migration schedules for Denmark by five-year age groups. However, the underlying factors that can shed light on the observed mortality trends received only little attention in his work.

Studies in historical demography indicate that the decline in mortality at the beginning of the 20th century is mainly due to a decline in mortality from infectious diseases; especially the decline in deaths from tuberculosis and diphtheria played an important role. Caselli, for example, argues that the decline in respiratory tuberculosis accounted for over half the gains in life expectancy between 1871 and 1911 in England and Italy (Schofield (Ed.) et al., 1991). Nevertheless, it is unrealistic to select these diseases as unique factors behind the mortality transition. The reductions in death rates from other infectious diseases such as the plaque, smallpox, cholera, typhus, typhoid fever, measles, whooping cough and malaria were also substantial and the decline in respiratory diseases such influenza, bronchitis and pneumonia also played a significant role. At the same time, mortality from diseases of the circulatory system and cancer increased, which led to a change in the structure of cause-specific mortality from infectious to degenerative diseases.

Data on cause-specific mortality for European countries of acceptable quality are available going back to about the middle of the 19th century. These data have been extensively exploited in historical demographic studies because of their accessibility. It is obvious that the examination of long-term trends in cause-specific mortality is only the first step in a demographic analysis, since the trends by themselves do not reveal the causative mechanisms of the mortality decline. In view of this fact, many explanations have been put forward. All of them are based largely on known facts and I will provide an overview of the most important ones.

McKeown (1976) argues that the mortality decline can be mainly attributed to improvements in nutrition during the 19th century. Nutrition seems to have a strong influence on the incidence, severity and lethality of such diseases as tuberculosis, bacterial diarrhoea, cholera, measles and, to some extent, diphtheria and influenza.

At the present time, malnutrition, especially protein-energy malnutrition, is thought to be linked to impairments of the immune system, particularly to the thymus gland and lymphoid tissues (Lunn in Schofield (Ed.) et al., 1991).

Other studies demonstrate that the decline in mortality took place chiefly due to improvements in the sanitary environment and public hygiene, which are usually associated with drainage and sewage disposal, a sufficient supply of safe drinking water, with clean and paved streets. The example of sewage conditions can be found in a survey of six European countries conducted by Thomas Legge (1896) in the earlier 1890s[10]. In Copenhagen, for example, the sewage disposal system was far from meeting the standards of the time: sewage conducted straight into the harbor. In addition, in some sections of Christiania (district of Copenhagen) drainage and pavement had not been completed. Johansen and Boje (1986) provided another example of living conditions in Odense at the beginning of the 19th century, where sewage flowed down the street into a trench. They described the conditions in Hans Jensens Stræde, where H. C. Anderson was born and where H. C. Anderson Hus (city museum) is now located. Today this street is the biggest tourist attraction in Odense.

Public health measures and effective governmental interventions also played a significant role. A classic example is the outbreak of cholera in Hamburg in 1892. The epidemic affected at least 16,926 of a total population of 625,000, and more than 8,605 people died of the disease (officially reported numbers). In contrast, only six cholera deaths were reported in Bremen. The number of cholera deaths in Hamburg exceed the number of deaths from this disease in all previous epidemics together. The local government was completely responsible for the epidemic in that it ignored the first cases of the disease, so as not to disrupt trade and business life in the city. The population was not informed about protective measures recommended by Koch (in fact, no proper attention was paid to his instructions against cholera at all). In contrast, the medical authorities in Bremen were convinced about Koch's recent discoveries and of the effectiveness of protective measures such as quarantine, isolation, water and milk boiling, hand disinfecting, and the avoidance of crowding. Before the epidemic, a hospital had been built in Bremerhaven and a disinfection plant was acquired. When the disease struck, the population was immediately informed about protective measures and the proper instructions were distributed. The results are self-evident (Bourdelais, P.; Woods, R. in Schofield (Ed.) et al., 1991).

Another group of factors, which is frequently discussed in connection with the decline in mortality, is the rising standard of living and improvements in housing and

---

[10] Woods, Robert. Public Health and Public Hygiene. In Schofield (Ed.) et al., 1991; 233-247.

working conditions. Dr. Edward Smith (1876) wrote: '… the peasant, gaining immunity from his open-air existence, may escape the noxious results of stagnant drains and even of impure water; but it is his sleeping accommodation which produces the most insidious (and often fatal) results upon his health. Overcrowding has probably killed more than all other evil conditions whatever.'[11] Improvements in housing conditions have usually been accompanied by legislative acts, which set the standards for new buildings, e.g., the Housing Act of 1858 in Denmark or the Act of 1902 in France. On the other hand, mortality was consistently lower in rural than in urban areas despite the generally worse housing conditions. The main reason seems to be that peasants spent most of their time working outside in the fresh air, so their exposure to environmental hazards was lower than for town workers. It has been suggested 'that the house itself was not the principle determining factor' and that there are other factors which are closely linked with poor housing conditions such as poor sanitation, malnutrition, etc. (John Burnett)[11].

Advances in medical science also played an important role in mortality decline. The introduction of a vaccine against smallpox in 1796 by Edward Jenner, the isolation of quinine in 1820 by Caventon and Pelletier (malaria treatment), Koch's discovery of the bacterial nature of cholera in 1884, the work of Behring on an immunization against diphtheria, the discoveries of Louis Pasteur, which had a profound influence on public health through the establishment of principles of pasteurization, antisepsis and asepsis - all these advances contributed indisputably to the observed mortality decline.

The role of medical intervention seems, however, to be less significant than the dissemination of medical knowledge and rules of public hygiene among people. For example, McKeown (1976) argued that advances in medical science cannot be credited as being the principle factor responsible for the decline in mortality since many diseases were already declining long before effective medical therapy had become available. The first antidiphtheritic serum was available in Denmark in the summer of 1895, but Thorvald Madsen (1956), who helped to prepare the serum, noted that the mortality rates had already fallen before it had become available. In view of this fact, Madsen and Madsen (1956) attributed the decline in mortality from this disease in the years around 1895 to changes in the type of diphtheria bacillus rather than to the introduction of serum therapy (Lancaster, p110, 1990). Jean N. Biraben in his work *Pasteur, Pasteurization, and Medicine* (in Schofield (Ed.) et al., 1991) states 'In Western Europe mortality had begun to fall during the 1870s, but its decline reached unprecedented levels from 1885 onwards. As it is clear …, it was not

---

[11] Burnett, John. Housing and the Decline of Mortality. In Schofield (Ed.) et al., 1991.

vaccines or sera which were responsible for this fall that has continued into our own period, but the spread of cleanliness, disinfection, antisepsis and asepsis'.

Other factors, which have been put forward to explain the decline in mortality, are changes in disease virulence, changes in climate, rising levels of social income and even the influence of sun activity. Attempts to separate factor-specific influence and to assign some numeric measure to the contribution of each individual factor to the decline in mortality are hampered by the lack of reliable data and the gap in knowledge about causative mechanisms. All historical demographers seem to agree that this is an unrealistic and futile task.

There have been less published on historical Danish developments than on other countries despite the rich volume of statistical data. Death counts by cause, for example, have been publishing for urban areas since 1860 and for the whole country since 1921. More scanty and less reliable data on causes of death can be found in parish reports (Johansen, 1996).

Andersen (1973) has put forward the agricultural reforms as the principal factor behind the decline in mortality from 1735 to 1839 (more modern periods have not been analyzed in his work). He also emphasizes the importance of economic growth, smallpox vaccination, and improvements in hygiene and housing conditions. He argues that hospitals did not contribute to the decline: on the contrary, admission to a hospital increased the risk of becoming infected.

Lancaster (1990) has maintained that the experience of Denmark is similar to that of most European countries, whereas the other Scandinavian countries should be treated as isolated areas. Unfortunately, this statement is not supported by any statistical material.

Our analysis of the Danish mortality surface suggests that the Danish population was among the mainstream of the late 19th century European mortality transitions. Moreover, there is some evidence that Denmark was ahead of many countries and that Danish gains in life expectancy were significantly higher than elsewhere. For example, Vallin (in Schofield (Ed.) et al., 1991) discusses life expectancy in different European countries on the eve of the First World War. It follows from his analysis that life expectancy in Denmark was the highest in Europe. Part of Vallin's table is reproduced in Table 3.2.

This statement is also supported by findings in Chapter 4, where Danish death rates are compared with mortality in other countries.

Table 3.2 Life expectancy in the beginning of the 20th century[12]

Country	Period	Life expectancy at birth
Denmark	1911–15	57.7
Norway	1911–21	57.2
Sweden	1911–20	57.0
Netherlands	1910–20	56.1
Ireland	1910–12	53.8
England and Wales	1910–11	53.5
Switzerland	1910–11	52.3
France	1908–13	50.4

3.2.4 Rates of mortality changes over time

In this section, we turn our attention to the rate of age-specific changes in death rates over time. The current rate of mortality change is an important indicator, since it shows the tendency of death rates to increase or decline. Information about rate of mortality change over time is frequently used in mortality and population projections. By using the data from the Danish mortality database, it is possible to estimate the surface of rates of mortality change over time and to reveal the age-year domains with different mortality trends. The Lexis map presented in Fig. 3.9, is quite new in demographic research in the way which it permits us to look at mortality changes over time.

The procedure used for estimating the surface of mortality change over time is described in Appendix 6. Using this procedure, rates of mortality change have been estimated for every year and age using 5 preceding and 5 following years. Thus, a single estimate of a rate of mortality change over time is based on 11 death rates centered at the year for which the estimate is produced. In Fig. 3.9, only the estimates based on the complete 11-year time series are shown, so the map only covers the period from 1840 to 1994, which is shorter than the period covered by the mortality database.

The scale shown on the right divides all estimates of rates of mortality change into four areas. Light gray (0–5) and light gray with diagonal fill (>5) depict the age-year domains in which death rates were increasing over time. Light gray (0–5) is used for areas with a rate of increase less than 5% and light gray with diagonal fill (>5) for areas with a rate of increase over 5%. Black (<-5) and dark gray with rectangle fill (-5–0) show areas with declining mortality. The rate of decline is less

---

[12] Reproduced from Vallin, J. in Schofield R. (Ed.) et al., 1991, p47.

than 5% for the dark gray area and more than 5% for the black area. The color white corresponds to the estimates, which were not significant at the 10% level or where the procedure could not produce an estimate because of a lack of the data.

We turn now to the discussion of the main features of these Lexis maps. The black blur at ages 0–15 and in the years around 1900 marks the onset of the persistent mortality decline in the Danish population. We can see that the high rates of improvement in reduction of mortality became evident in the early 1890s, both in the male and female populations. Prior to that time mortality changes were of a sporadic nature, with distinctly expressed periods of increasing and declining mortality. The rates of improvement were highest (> 5%) at ages 1–15, with a peak 8–10% at about age 5. Progress of up to 2.5% per year is also evident at ages up to 40 in the female population and up to 30 in the male population. At higher ages the improvements were less significant.

Over time the area with high rates of improvements in reduction of death rates spread out to higher ages, and rates of progress above 5% are to be observed up to the age of 40 and until the middle of the 1950s. This drastic mortality decline was interrupted only twice during these 60 years: first by the influenza epidemic of 1918 and second by the Second World War. The pattern of mortality decline at ages below 40 was similar for males and females - but not above this age. After 40 appreciable mortality progress (1–5%) can be observed in the periods 1900–1920 and 1940–1950 for males and in 1935–1960 for females.

Starting in the 1960s, the mortality decline decelerated significantly, and there was even some mortality increase, as indicated by the light gray, clearly visible on the maps. An especially strong rise in male mortality (1.5%) is to be seen in the period 1955–1970 and at ages 55–75. I conclude that the late 1950s mark the start of stagnation in the Danish mortality decline at adult ages (<70).

Rather surprising, stagnation in death rates was not uniform over age. During this period, striking progress in the reduction of death rates can be observed at older ages. Especially eye-catching is the mortality decline (about 2%) in the female population at ages 70–95 in the period 1940–1990. The rate of decline in the male population was less significant: a comparable level of decline is visible only in the years surrounding 1970. The highest rates of progress in reduction of the oldest-old mortality are found in the period 1965–1969, where the rate of progress at age 80 was about 3% for males and 5% for females.

In the late 1980s, another change in the dynamics of death rates took place. Male mortality at ages 50–80 started to decline while female mortality at ages 60–80 began to increase. In addition, the rate of mortality decline at older ages fell to zero, indicating the onset of stagnation in oldest-old mortality. In view of the importance of progress made in the reduction of death rates at advanced ages for the projection of the oldest-old population, I computed, separately for males and females, standardized death rates for ages 80 and over. A survey of mortality trends for the period 1990–1999 shows that in both populations, the death rates remained at a constant level after the year 1985. Only starting in 1995, can a slight decline in the death rates be observed.

To complete the account of mortality change over time, cohort lines have been added to Fig. 3.9. One can see that the female mortality increase runs along the cohorts born around the year 1920. In the male population, a similar effect is noticeable for the cohorts born around 1950. This pattern is clearly observed and it calls for explanation. So far there have been no demographic studies, which link the rate of mortality change over time to events that occurred earlier in life and to cohort-specific characteristics.

3.2.5 Sex ratio of mortality

As described above, the decline in mortality in recent decades was greater for the female than for the male population. In order to examine the sex differences in survival more closely, a surface of sex ratios of Danish mortality was estimated (Fig. 3.10). The mortality ratio surface was computed with the kernel estimation procedure (Appendix 7), using a 3x3 smoothing matrix and Epanechnikov bivariate kernel weights. At boundaries where no complete data for smoothing are available - that is, at age zero and in the years 1835 and 1999 - the ratio of age-specific death rates was plotted instead of kernel estimates. The Lexis map shown in Fig. 3.10 allows us to combine both qualitative depiction of male-female survival differences and quantitative information about the extent of excess male mortality in recent period.

The scale divides the surface into 6 areas. The light gray (0.8–1.0) and light gray with rectangle fill (<0.8) are used to depict the excess of female mortality, while others are used for the areas with excess male mortality. The level of equal mortality in two populations can be followed with the contour line at level 1.

The black (>1.80) area, for example, comprises ratios where male death rates were 80% higher than female.

As can be seen in Fig. 3.10, there are three distinct periods with clearly different patterns of male-female mortality differences. Until the 1920s, females had a mortality disadvantage at ages 5–20 and 25–40 with the excess mortality of about 20%. This can be largely attributed to the complications in connection with childbearing. On the other hand, the excess of male mortality is to be observed in infancy, in the earlier twenties and at ages over 40. The most significant differences were found at ages 45–65, where male death rates outnumbered female rates by about 20–50%.

This pattern of survival was remarkably stable over a period of 90 years. The first signs of changes in the mortality differences between sexes did not start to become evident until the early 1920s. The period from 1920 to 1950 is characterized by minimal sex differences in mortality. Even if female mortality was generally lower than male mortality, the sex ratios fall within the 20% range, which makes this period remarkable in that there was a high degree of similarity in the mortality regimes of both populations.

The end of the Second World War, clearly marks the onset of new regime in the sex differences in mortality. Already in 1950, male death rates outnumbered female rates at virtually all ages. Especially high differences are to be observed at ages 50–60 and at ages close to 20. These two age groups acted as starting points for two areas of excess male mortality that emerged later in time: one at adult ages and another at young adult ages. Both areas are colored black (>1.8), which corresponds to an excess of male mortality of over 80%.

At the young ages, the area with excessive male mortality has been spreading over time to cover more ages. At present time it encompasses the age group 15–40. For comparison, in 1950 excess male mortality of more than 80% occurred only at ages 18–23.

In the age group 50–60, the gap between male and female mortality rose over time, simultaneously moving to the higher ages, i.e. somewhat along the cohort lines. The sex differences reached a peak in 1980 at age 70, and then declined. In this period, male death rates were approximately double those of females. Toward the 1990s, the area with the highest excess of male mortality disappeared completely. This pattern is clearly demonstrated by eye-catching black ellipse in the upper right-hand corner of Fig. 3.10.

The decline in sex differences at ages 60–80 was the main reason for a convergence in life expectancies for the male and female populations of Denmark in recent years. Death rates at young and young adult ages are very low nowadays and changes in these rates affect life expectancy at birth in a less notable way. The convergence in life expectancies can also be observed in other countries as well. To reveal the age-specific mortality differences, I have produced similar mortality-sex-ratio maps for Canada (Andreev, 2000), the Netherlands and Sweden (unpublished). It turns out that the global pattern of mortality ratios is strikingly similar between countries. There are still some differences between the maps, but there are far more similarities to be observed. It might be the case that there are certain factors that

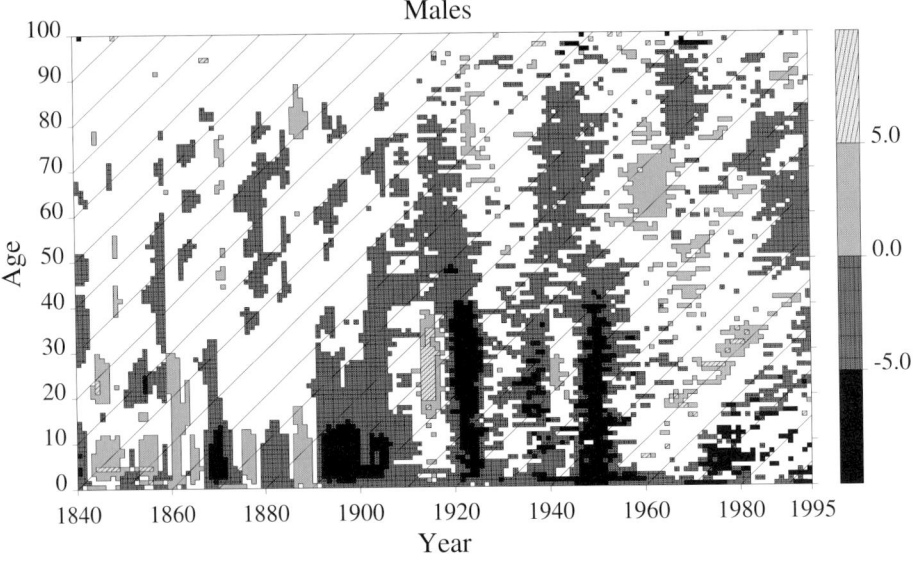

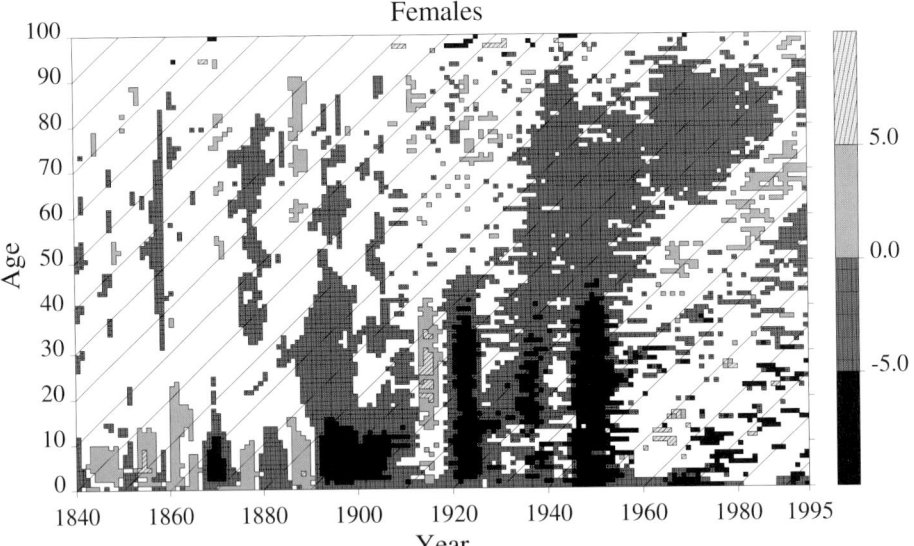

Rates of mortality change over time have been estimated by
fitting a regression model to 11-years series of death rates.
Only estimates based on complete series and significant at the 10% level are shown.

Figure 3.9. Rate of Danish mortality changes over time

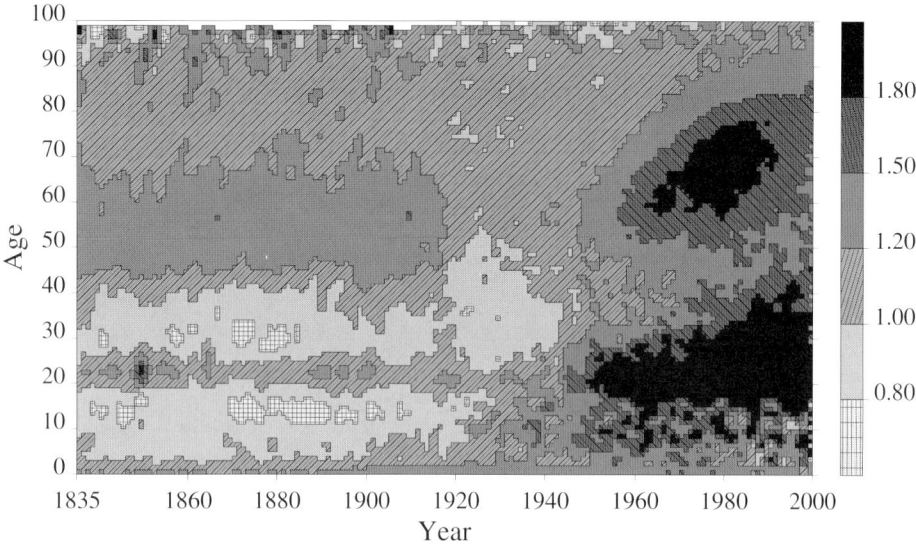

Smoothed with 3x3 bivariate Epanechnikov kernel.

Figure 3.10. Sex ratio of Danish mortality

affect mortality in some uniform way, thereby maintaining the fixed pattern of male-female differences over various countries.

3.2.6 Compression of mortality

Other important insights into Danish mortality evolution can be gained by studying compression of mortality over age and time. There is a lively debate in the demographic literature about whether or not the maximal life span of humans is fixed and whether or not there has been a rectangularization of the survival curve in recent decades (e.g. Fries, 1980; Aarssen and de Haan, 1994; Kannisto et. al., 1994; Curtsinger, et. al., 1992). The data from the Danish mortality database allow us to investigate the dynamics of the mortality compression over age and time by examining trends in the distribution of life table deaths for the period of 165 years. Such undertaking is the first of its kind in demographic research for the studying of mortality compression.

To produce the Lexis maps shown in Fig. 3.11, the d_x columns were extracted from set of period life tables and plotted as a Lexis map. The death distribution surface has been also smoothed on a 3x3 matrix with weights generated by bivariate Epanechnikov kernel (Appendix 5).

The scale legend shows the percentage levels of the death distribution. All values of d_x falling in the same range are plotted with the same color and filling pattern as depicted by the scale. For example, the maximum of female death distribution at older ages in 1835 is observed at age 74; the percentage of life table deaths at this age is about 1.66% (dark gray area (1.5–2)). In 1999, the maximum is at age 87, where the proportion of deaths is 3.6% (dark gray area with vertical fill (3.3–3.8)).

To emphasize the evolution of the maximum of the death distribution at older ages, the white line connecting the ages with the maximal proportions of the life table deaths was added to the maps. Since we are concerned with the compression of mortality, the maximum of the death distribution at adult ages has been stressed rather than infant mortality.

As is evident from Fig. 3.11, the mode of life table death distribution at older ages has increased substantially since the middle of the 19th century. For males, it has increased from 70 to 78 years of age and for females from 73 to 87 (1.5 times higher than for males). However, the pattern of increase was not parallel for both sexes. The main increase in the mode of males occurred before 1940. There have been no significant changes since that year. For the female population the increase has been more persistent over time and has even accelerated since 1940.

The pattern of mortality compression is also clearly revealed by Fig. 3.11. The areas in light gray (0.1–0.2) and light gray with rectangle fill (<0.1) in the lower right-hand corner correspond to exceptionally low levels of death density. In the period 1970–1999, the number of life table deaths below age 50 was about 8% for males and 5% for females, whereas in the 19th century these numbers were 46% and 44%, respectively. If we exclude deaths at age 0, the difference is still marked: 7% vs. 35% for males and 4% vs. 35% for females. This huge difference resulted from the rapid progress in the reduction of mortality of children and young adults (Fig. 3.9). Progress at high ages has been less dramatic. Undoubtedly, this pattern of mortality decline led to a compression of the death distribution at age about 80, which prevailed until the mid-1960s for both males and females. As more and more deaths have become concentrated at ages close to 80, new domains of high death density have emerged on the Lexis maps. In Fig. 3.11, these areas appear in black (>3.8) for females and dark gray with vertical fill (3.3–3.8) for males. Contour lines 3.30 and 3.80 circumscribe ages and years with the highest density of life table deaths ever observed in Danish population.

However, along with the process of mortality compression, the proportion of deaths at very old ages has increased as well. On the Lexis maps, this is indicated by the rising contour lines at age 80 and above. Until the 1960s, mortality decline at the

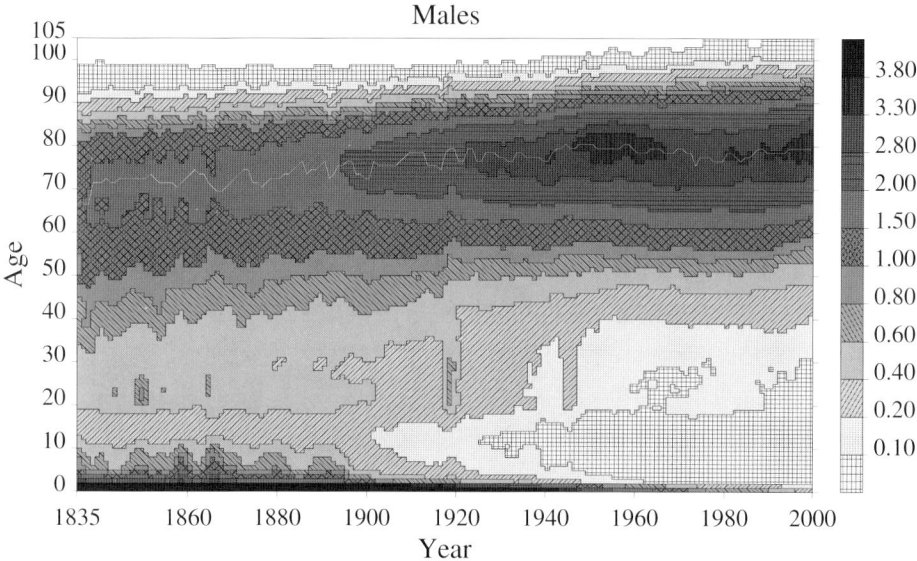

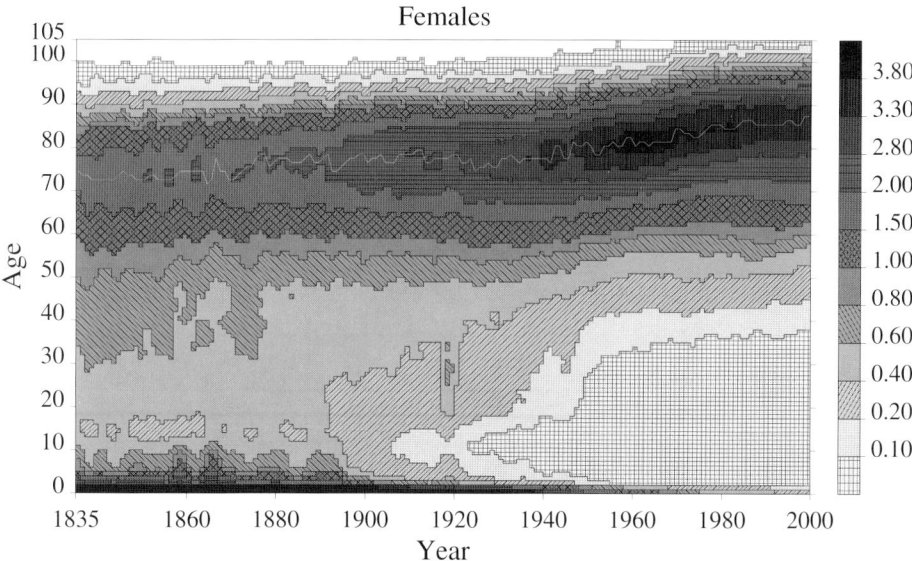

Smoothed with 3x3 bivariate Epanechnikov kernel.

Figure 3.11. Danish life table death distribution (%)

highest ages was negligible compared with that in the lower age groups. The death distribution was becoming more and more compressed at age about 80 despite the increasing proportion of deaths at ages 80 and above. Starting with the late 1960s, mortality reductions at age 70 and above became appreciable and had a profound influence on the tail of the death distribution. As a result, the area with the highest death density disappeared on both maps in the 1970s and the age at maximal death density moved toward the higher ages in the female population.

In the most recent years (1995–1999) due to reductions of death rates at ages below 70 in the male population (Fig. 3.8), the area with a high density of life table deaths started to emerge again, virtually at the same ages as in the period 1940–1960. In the female population, such phenomenon is not observed.

These findings are summarized in Table 3.3. The studied period has been divided into four time intervals and the proportion of life table deaths computed for ages below 75, 75–85 and for age 85 and over. The phenomenon described in the previous paragraphs is manifested in the trends in the proportion of life table deaths in the age group 75–85. The proportion increased until the 1970s and then started to decline. The proportion of deaths in the lowest age group continuously declined and the proportion in the highest age group continuously increased.

Table 3.3 Proportions of the life table deaths in Denmark.

	Males			Females		
Period	0–75	75–85	85+	0–75	75–85	85+
1835–1900	81.5	14.4	4.1	77.0	16.9	6.1
1900–1950	64.1	26.1	9.9	60.0	28.1	11.9
1950–1970	51.4	32.5	16.1	40.4	36.8	22.7
1970–1995	50.4	31.4	18.2	33.3	31.8	34.9

Other important insights can be gained by exploring some measure of uncertainty or dispersion of period survival functions conditional on age instead of plotting directly life table death distributions. Entropy of a probability distribution seems to serve this purpose well as it approaches zero if deaths are concentrated in a narrow age interval and it uniformly increases if occurrence of deaths becomes more and more spread over ages. Thus lower levels of entropy correspond to higher levels of compression of death distribution. If we look at Fig. 3.11, year 1960 it is clear that compression of female death distribution is higher than male. For example, area with the highest death density (>3.80) is to be observed in female map but not in male. Computing entropy of life table death distribution for year 1960 yields 3.98 for males and 3.87

for females, which corresponds well to our expectations.

Fig. 3.12 shows estimates of entropy of all survival distributions for period from 1835–1999. For each year and age, I computed the entropy of the respective period survival functions conditional on age and plotted them in a form of a Lexis map. For males, for example, entropy at age 50 in 1960 is equal to 3.7 and it corresponds to the entropy of the life table death distribution estimated for ages 50 and above and for year 1960.

Entropy at age 0 (bottom line in Fig. 3.12) corresponds to all ages and summarizes the survival experience of the complete life span - much the same as the life expectancy at birth - but its meaning is an uncertainty of the life table death distribution, rather than the expected moment of death. We can see that until 1930, the entropy at age 0 belongs to the areas with the highest values observed on the maps (>4.1 and 4.0–4.1). Uncertainty of the moment of death is respectively the highest for this period and compression of death distribution is lowest. Over time, the entropy at age 0 declines reaching a minimum in the 1960s. If we look at age 0 in the year 1960, it belongs to the area (3.9–4.0) for males and to the area (3.8–3.9) for females. Exact numbers are 3.98 and 3.87, respectively. This is a manifestation of compression of *complete* life table death distribution, which was the highest during this period. This is also consistent with the previous finding, because the 1960s are the years characterized by the appearance of an area with the highest death densities (Fig. 3.11).

Afterwards entropy at age 0, starts to increase again and the death distribution becomes more uncertain and less compressed. In the year 1990, it reaches a level of 4.00 for males and 3.94 for females. The life table death distribution spreads out over age during this period, which is attributed to the decline of death rates at oldest-old ages. Recall that the rates of mortality decline at ages 70 and over were the highest during the period 1960–1990 (Fig. 3.9). The gains in entropy at age 0 were also higher for females than for males over this period, and it is consistent with the fact that progress in reduction of death rates at advanced ages was higher for females (Fig. 3.9).

In recent years (1990–1999), the entropy at age 0 started to decline again. It follows from Fig. 3.12, because the area (4.0–4.1) disappeared in the male population and the area (3.9–4.0) shrunk in the population of females. Thus in recent years, the Danish death distribution becomes more compressed than before, similar to what we observed in the 1960s. Again, it can be explained by the dynamics of the death rates over this period. From Fig. 3.9, it is evident that this period is characterized by the reduction of death rates at the middle ages, especially at ages

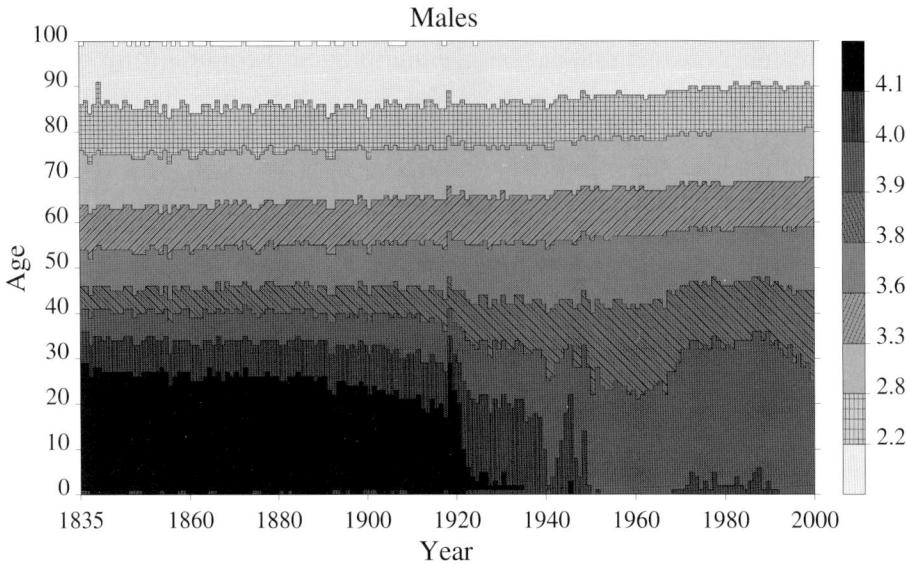

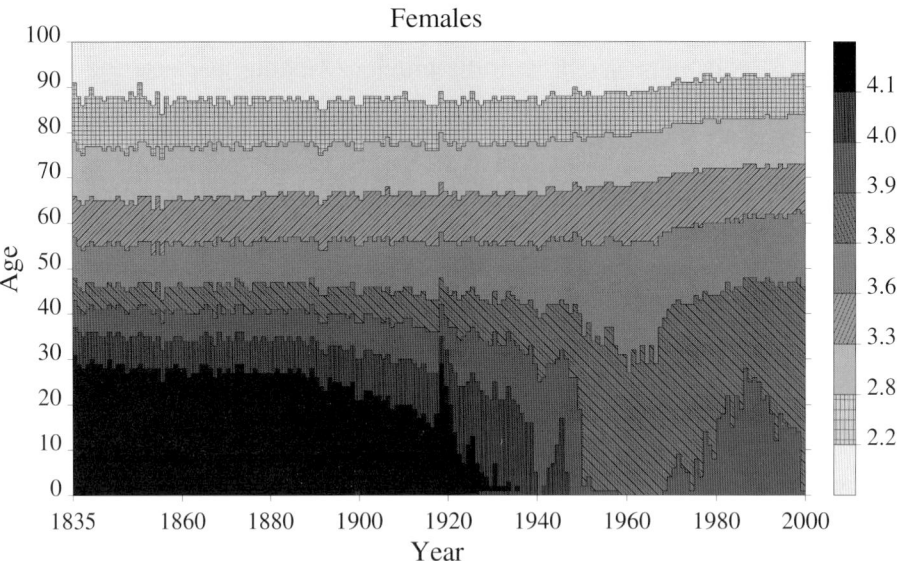

Figure 3.12. Entropy of Danish life table death distribution

from 50 to 70. On the other hand progress in reduction of mortality at oldest-old ages is negligible. This leads to compression of death distribution.

A similar pattern of entropy changes over time is to be observed at ages up to 50. That is if we compute the entropy of death distribution for ages 50 and over (or for any age in the range 0–50) and for every calendar year, time trends in this quantity will generally follow the pattern observed for age 0.

At the higher ages the pattern is completely different. If we look at ages above 50 in Fig. 3.12, we can see that the contour lines at these age have been steadily increasing over time, pointing to the fact that the entropy at these ages has been also increasing. Thus, at higher ages there is no compression of mortality is to be observed.

To summarize, the findings from Danish mortality data suggest that the compression of mortality is an outcome of complex interactions between the reductions in death rates in different age groups. Mortality developments over the 19th and first half of 20th century led to a compression of death distribution, which reached its peak in the 1960s. After that time, the decline in oldest-old mortality became appreciable and proportions of deaths at oldest-old ages rose substantially reducing the level of compression. In recent years, due to the developments in the death rates at adult ages compression of death distribution resumes again, especially for males.

The age with the highest death density (second mode of life table death distribution) has been gradually increasing over time, especially in the female population. For males the mode of death distribution stagnated in the 1940s and even declined in the later 1970s. In the last decade there has been a slight increase.

4. A comparison of mortality in Denmark and other developed countries

4.1 Introduction

The analysis of the Danish population fulfilled in the previous chapter allowed us to investigate the evolution of the Danish population over age and time. More or less comparable data are also available for several developed countries, which makes it possible to explore the evolution of the Danish population from the international perspective. In this chapter, I present and discuss the age- and time-specific surfaces of the ratio of death rates in Denmark and several other developed countries. This permits us to reveal the age specific differences in Danish survival and to follow their development over time.

The analysis is based on a comparison of Danish death rates with mortality in the following nine countries: Austria, Canada, England and Wales, Finland, France, Japan, Netherlands, Norway and Sweden. Data for all nine countries originate from the publications of the National Statistical Offices for various years. The official data are not usually completely suitable for estimating the death rates by single year and age, in particular for the earlier years, which requires additional labor similar to that involved in the construction of the Danish mortality database. Wherever relevant, I will provide a brief overview of the data compilation procedures for the countries included in the analysis.

The procedure for estimating the surface of a ratio of death rates in two countries is the same as that used to produce the sex ratio of the Danish mortality (Fig. 3.10) and is given in Appendix 7. Here, however, I did not apply any smoothing techniques, the ratio of death rates at any given year and age is based only on the two death rates in the compared populations. The level of statistical significance has been chosen to be 10% and the only statistically significant estimates of the death rate ratios have been plotted in the Lexis maps included in this chapter. Printed versions of the death rate ratio maps are black and white and those included on the accompanying CD-ROM are in color.

4.2 Denmark to Sweden

The core set of the Swedish mortality data has been compiled by Hans Lundström. Later, the Swedish database has been extended and added to the Berkley mortality database[13] (BMD) by John Wilmoth. The procedures used for assembling and

---

[13] http://www.demog.berkeley.edu/wilmoth/mortality/

producing the population estimates can be found on the BMD web site. Data for the recent years have been added from the statistical publications of Statistics of Sweden by the author. It is also worth noting that Swedish death counts are available by single year of age from 1861 onwards, while Danish data in such detail have been available only since the beginning of the 20th century.

The ratio of death rates in Denmark and Sweden, over all periods with available data is given in Figure 4.1. The scale shown on the right includes seven levels, which seems to be a reasonable choice for representing the Lexis maps of death rate ratios. Scales with more levels, will inevitable bring more details to view on account of impairing the perception of global patterns. On the other hand, a smaller number of levels provides a much too simple presentation of the observed patterns. After some experimenting with the different scale levels, its number was chosen to be seven. The actual levels of contours run from 0.55 to 1.82 at multiples of 1.22 passing through the point of equity. Using a constant coefficient of 1.22, permits us to preserve the same pattern of death rate ratios whenever the ratio of Danish to Swedish or Swedish to Danish death rates is shown in the Lexis map. If one decides to plot a ratio of Swedish to Danish death rates, instead of Danish to Swedish as in the Figure 4.1, the Lexis map areas will swap around the point of equity, but the pattern shown in Figure 4.1 will be exactly the same. For example, the area (>1.82) in Figure 4.1 will appear as area (<0.55) on the new map, the area (1.49–1.82) will appear as the area (0.55–0.67) et cetera.

The areas of the Lexis map are colored with gray hues from light to black with light gray areas representing the excess of Swedish mortality and dark gray areas displaying the excess of Danish mortality. For example, the areas painted in black correspond to ages and years where death rates in the Danish population were more then 1.82 times higher (or 80%) than those in the Swedish population. Sometimes it is difficult to distinguish between the two adjacent gray hues, so I have added three filling patterns to simplify the perception of the different Lexis map areas.

The main advantage of such a presentation of survival differences in two populations, is that we can immediately see at glance where the death rates were significantly different between two populations and how such differences evolved over time. Figure 4.1 tells us that there are several distinct periods; each of them characterized by a certain pattern of difference in the age-specific death rates.

Until the year 1900, death rates at the ages below 10 years were generally higher in Sweden, while the Swedish death rates at older ages were on an average lower, especially in the age groups 10–40 for females and 10–20 for males. At the beginning of the 20th century, the pattern abruptly changed. The Danish death rates

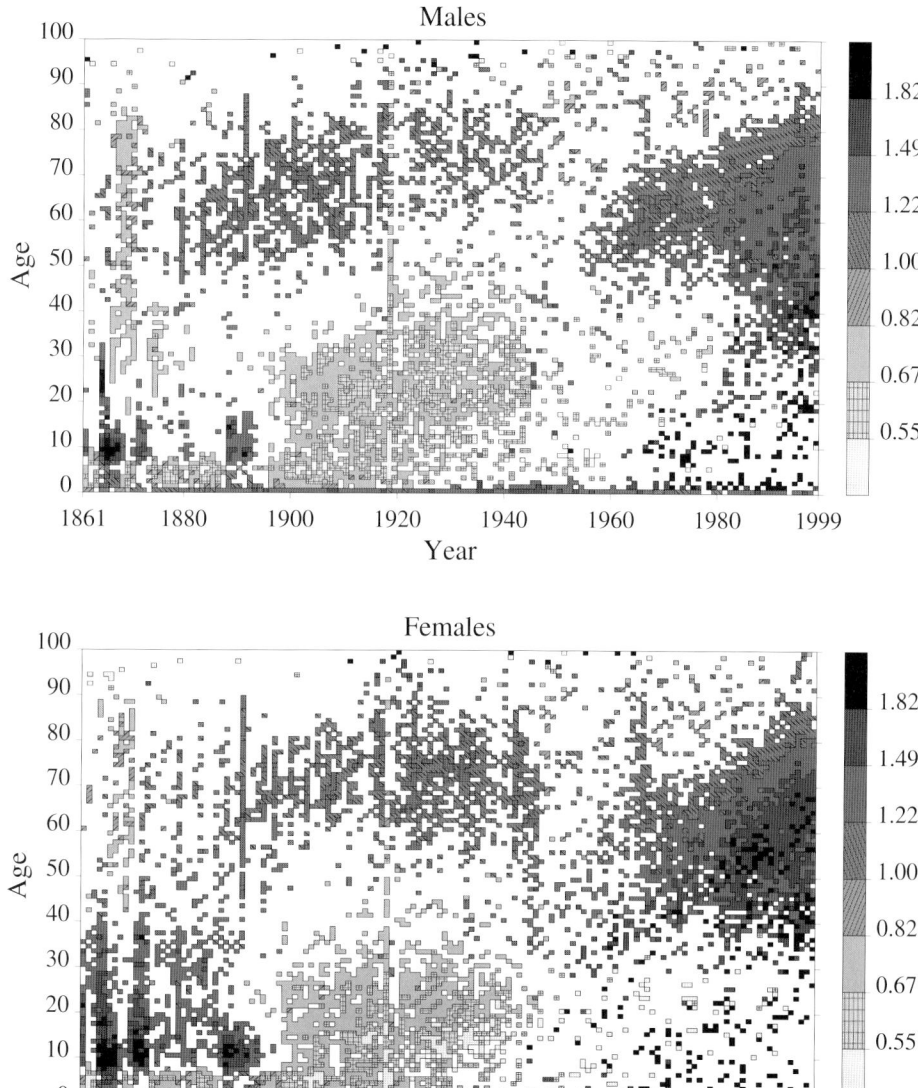

Figure 4.1. Ratio of death rates, Denmark to Sweden

are lower for ages up to 40 years, except for the infant death rates. The excess of Swedish mortality was about 20–50% and was more pronounced in the female population. In the age group 40–60, the death rates in two countries were almost the same, but the Danish death rates were generally higher for the older ages and also for infants. The difference of the death rates at older ages was however moderate, that is less than 20% for most of ages of this group.

The end of the WWII marks another change in the mortality regime of the two countries. Until 1960, mortality in both countries was virtually the same except in the case of infants. Higher death rates amongst infants are still to be observed in Denmark. Starting in the 1960s, the first signs of the excess of Danish mortality at ages close to 60 became evident. The pattern of excess Danish mortality in the population of males was sporadic, with values of about 20%. Starting in the 1980s, the situation worsened and the area of excess male mortality spread to the higher and lower ages. At the same time, the mortality difference at age 60 rose to 40%. Up until 1999, there was a tendency of augmentation of mortality differences between the populations and no reverse trends were clearly perceptible.

For the females, the onset of systematic excess mortality lies somewhat later than for males. With a high degree of confidence, we can point to the late 1960s as the time when the Danish female mortality started to outnumber Swedish mortality. The dynamics of this process is essentially the same as for males, i.e. the excess spread out to cover more ages and the differences in the middle of the excess mortality area were aggravating. However, the process was more rapid and led to higher mortality differences in the most recent years. In the year 1999, for example, excess female mortality at ages 55–75 was more than 50%, whereas no such level of excess is found in the male population.

4.3   Denmark to Norway

Data for Norway during the period 1846–1980 have been compiled by Jens-Kristian Borgan (1983). For the later years, comparable data have been obtained directly from Norway Statistics. The data for earlier periods are less comparable with Danish data, because the Norwegian death counts were classified by age and year of birth. Before the comparison was made, the data for Norway were separated evenly between Lexis triangles, which might introduce some additional bias in the estimation of age-specific death rates, because the Lexis triangles belong to different ages. How significant this is for the analysis performed here and how the separation procedure can be improved is a question for further investigation. At ages 80 and over, the population estimates have been computed by the extinct cohort method.

In general, the age-specific differences in Danish and Norwegian survival over age and time (Fig. 4.2) resemble those of the Danish-Swedish comparison (Fig. 4.1). There is, however, some significant deviation from the pattern described in the previous section. In the 19th century, for example, death rates at ages 50 and above were considerably lower in Norway than in Denmark, amounting to 20–50%. This is higher than we found when comparing Danish and Swedish mortality. At ages 10–50, the mortality in both countries was nearly the same except in the age group 20–30 for males, where the Danish death rates were in fact lower than Norwegian.

At the beginning of 20th century, the death rates of children and young adults (<50) declined more rapid in the Danish population creating an area with excess Norwegian mortality. In Figure 4.2, this area appears as a light gray spot in the middle of the maps. The excess of Norwegian mortality over this period was more pronounced than the Swedish mortality excess. For example, when comparing the males over the period 1895–1930 and in the age group 15–30, I found that the death rates in Norway were more than 80% higher than in Denmark. Such large differences were not observed between Denmark and Sweden. The devastating effects of WWII are also strikingly higher in Norway than in Denmark, especially for males.

In contrast with child and adult ages, Danish death rates at older ages (60–90) were higher than in Norway. This is essentially the pattern we found in the Danish-Swedish comparison, except that the Danish mortality excess was less notable in former case. On average, the death rates in two countries differ by a factor 1.2–1.5, which is higher than for Sweden over the same period.

The end of WWII brought mortality regimes in both counties very close to each other, especially that of males. For females, the change is less obvious, as the death rates at ages 60 and over were still significantly higher in Denmark than in Norway.

In the male population, the death rates were converging over time, up until the 1980s when an opposite trend took over. Similar to the Sweden, the Danish death rates at middle ages started to rise over time, forming an area with excess Danish mortality. Divergent trends in the death rates of both countries were less marked than compared to Sweden and on average an area with excess Danish mortality is less noticeable.

In the female populations, the relative dynamics of the death rates in Norway and Denmark was to a large extent similar to those observed in the Danish-Swedish comparison. An area with excess Danish mortality started to form at age 50 in the late 1960s and it spread out over time to cover more ages later. Contrary to the unfavorable trends in Danish mortality at adult ages, death rates at older ages were

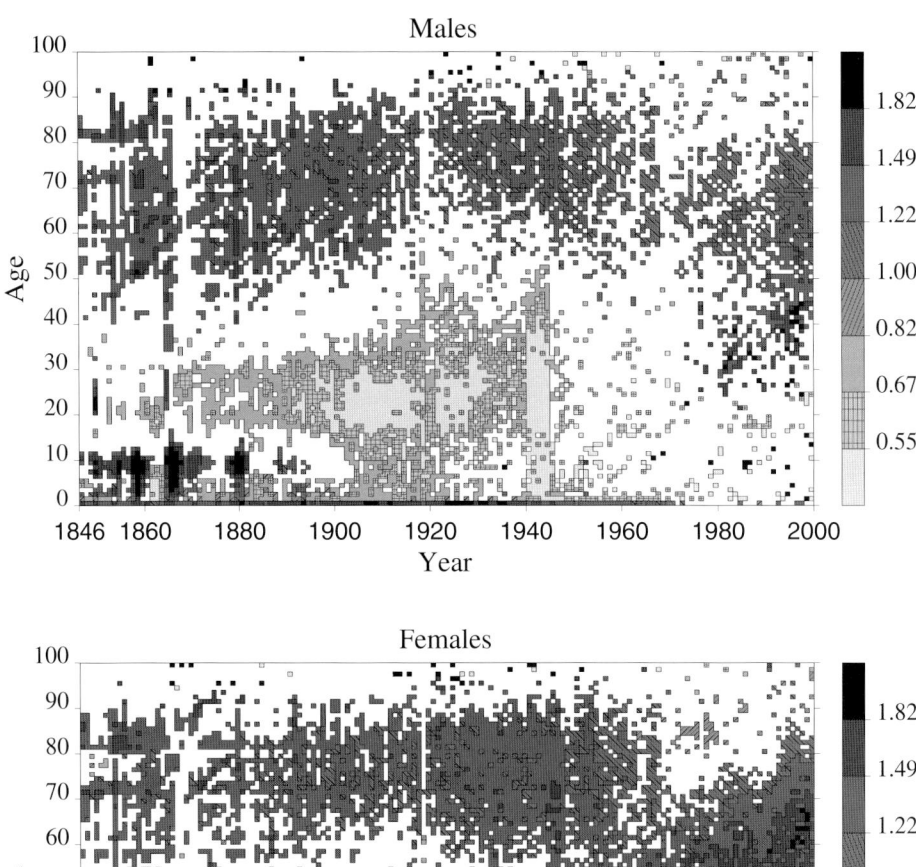

Figure 4.2. Ratio of death rates, Denmark to Norway

declining faster in Denmark than in Norway. Earlier differences in mortality between the females of Denmark and Norway at older ages (>75) disappeared after the late 1960s and in the age group 80–90, they were even significantly lower in Denmark during the period 1970–1980. In Figure 4.2, this area appears in light gray with a right diagonal fill pattern. In recent years, however, this Danish advantage has been largely lost.

4.4 Denmark to Finland

Finland was the last Nordic country included in the comparison. The population data is a combination of the data sets obtained directly from Statistics of Finland and the Finnish databases included in the Kannisto-Thatcher database on old age mortality maintained by the Max Planck Institute for Demographic Research, Germany. The population estimates at ages 80 and over have been computed by the extinct cohort method.

Figure 4.3 reveals that the death rates in the male population of Finland have been significantly higher for virtually all ages during the period 1941–1980. Especially striking is the excess of Finish mortality observed during WWII and the following years thereafter. The death rates among young adults (ages 20–40), have been higher by a factor of 10–30, and by a of factor 2–10 at older ages. Over time, convergence in death rates occurred in both populations and by the year 1980 Finnish death rates were higher by only 20–50%. In the following years after 1980, the process of convergence continued, and the Finnish death rates at ages 60–80 fell to levels even lower than the male population of Denmark. Mortality at ages 15–60 in Finland, is still slightly higher than in Denmark, and the oldest-old ages (>80) levels of mortality in both countries are very close to each other.

The relative dynamics of the death rates in the populations of females has been quite different than that of males. During the period of 1941–1950, the female death rates have been considerably higher in Finland than in Denmark, but the excess of the female mortality was not as striking as in case of the males. On average, they were higher by a factor 2–5. To a large extent, by the mid-1960s, the death rates of the two population converged, with the exception of the older ages (>65), where Finnish female death rates were still higher by 20–30%. At the beginning of the 1970s, due to the rapid decline of the Finnish death rates, an area with excess Danish mortality started to form at ages close to 50. Over time, the excess of Danish mortality spread to cover more ages, simultaneously aggravating in the middle. This is the essential pattern we found when comparing Danish female mortality with the mortality in Sweden and Norway.

At older ages (>70), the death rates in Denmark continued to stay at lower

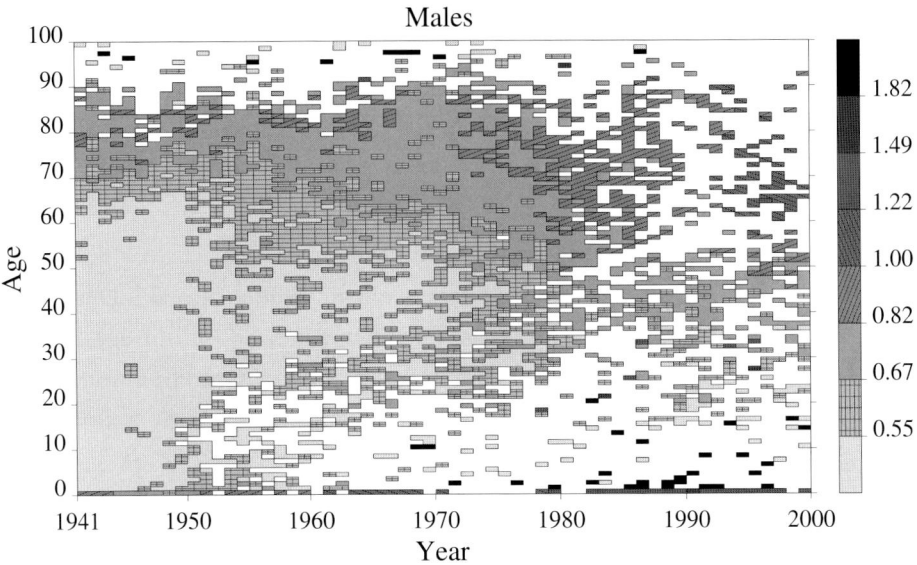

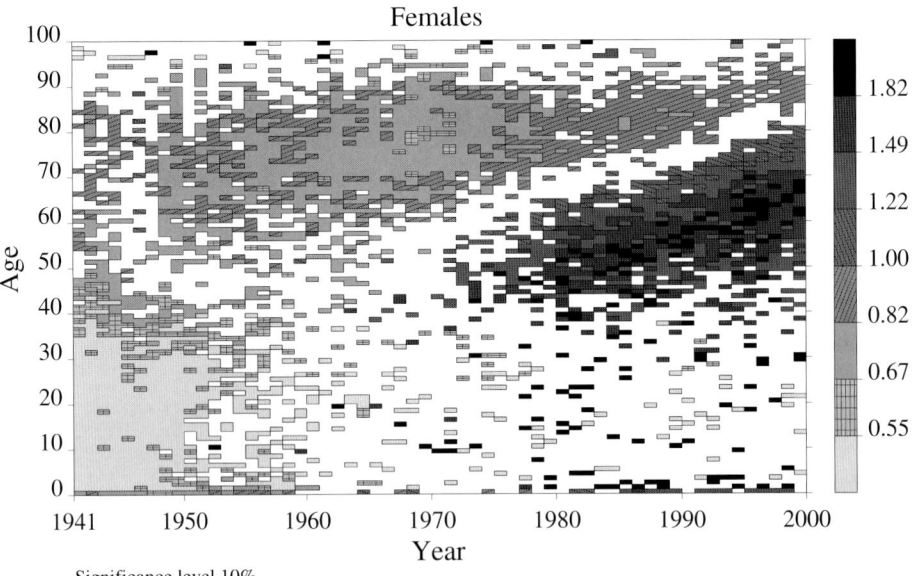

Significance level 10%

Figure 4.3. Ratio of death rates, Denmark to Finland

levels until the present time, but the age group with the lower mortality has been inevitably shrinking due to unfavorable developments at lower ages. In the year 1999, Danish death rates were only lower at ages 85 and over and the excess of Finnish mortality at these ages was about 5–10%.

4.5 Denmark to the Netherlands

The data for the Netherlands begin at in 1850 and have been assembled in a mortality database by E. Tabeau (Tabeau et. al. 1994). The data for recent years have been obtained directly from Statistics Netherlands. The missing data for some years, has also been acquired from the Kannisto-Thatcher database. For the population at ages 80 and above, as in case with other countries, the data has been computed by the extinct cohort method.

Figure 4.4 shows the results of the comparison of the Danish and Dutch mortality. The excess of Danish mortality in the 19th century, was at ages 5–15, but at all the other ages, mortality in Denmark was lower than in the Netherlands. Over the period 1900–1960, death rates were very close in both countries, except for the population under 10 years of age. There, the Danish death rates were significantly lower than the Dutch. For ages 20–50 years, the Danish mortality was slightly higher than the Dutch. The devastating effects of the influenza epidemics during 1918 and especially of WWII, have been more profound in the population of the Netherlands. These effects are indicated in Figure 4.4 by two vertical lines in light gray during the respective years.

Since the end of the Second World War, relative developments in the death rates of the two countries fit to the Swedish-Danish pattern. We can see how the areas with excess Danish mortality started to grow in the 1960s at approximately the age of 50 for females and 30 for males. Over time, they spread out to other ages, producing an excess of Danish mortality for virtually all ages, from 30 to 80, in the year 1999. For females, the highest differences are found at ages from 50 to 70, while for males from 30 to 50. Positive trends in the Danish death rates are not perceptible until the recent years.

4.6 Denmark to Austria

To compare Danish and Austrian death rates over age and time, the Statistical Office of Austria was contacted and the data was received for the period after 1947. Population estimates at the highest ages were not available by single age group and so they have been estimated by the extinct cohort method.

The pattern of Danish-Austrian mortality difference (Fig. 4.5) resembles the pattern found in the Danish-Finnish comparisons. In the late 1940s and in the 1950s,

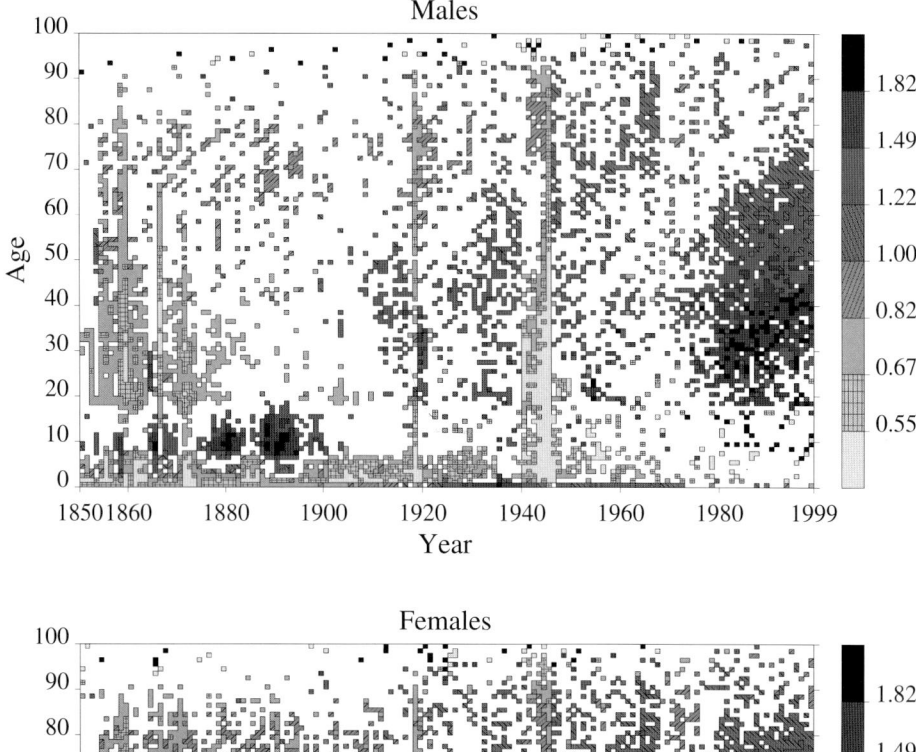
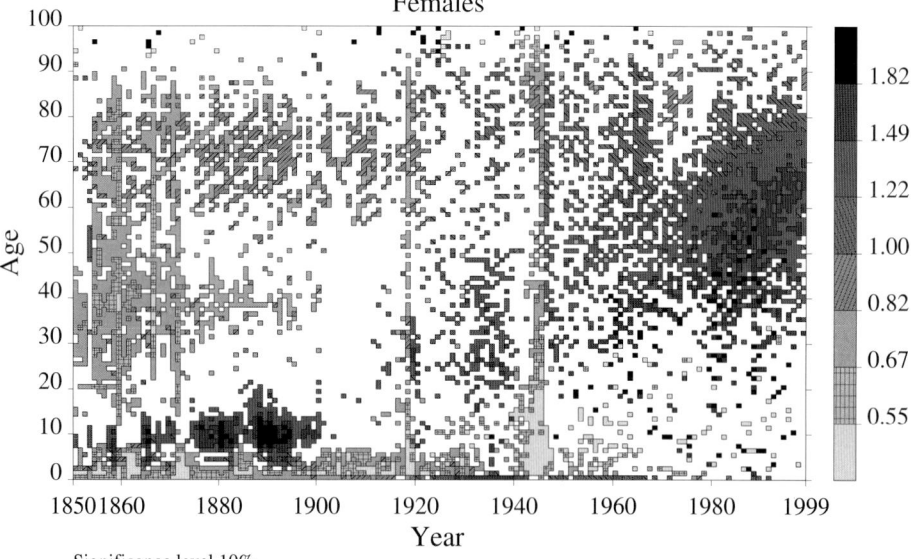

Significance level 10%

Figure 4.4. Ratio of death rates, Denmark to the Netherlands

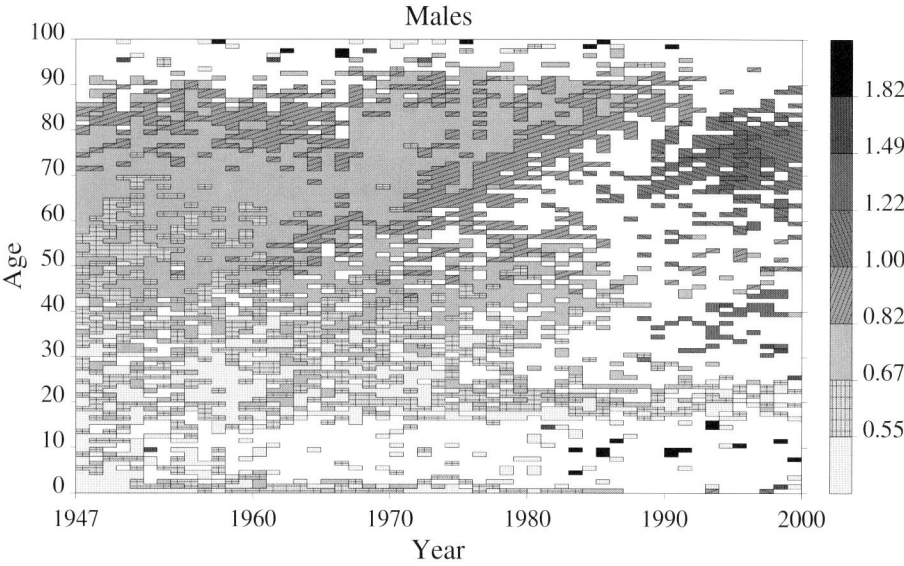

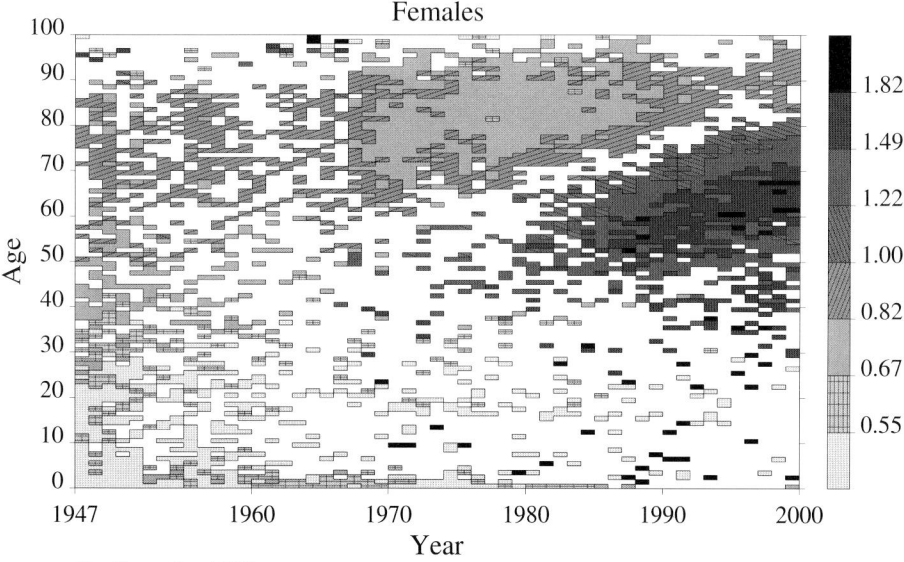

Significance level 10%

Figure 4.5. Ratio of death rates, Denmark to Austria

Austrian death rates were significantly higher than Danish for virtually all ages. Especially large differences in death rates are to be observed in the populations of males. Over time, death rates in Austria declined faster than in Denmark, surpassing the Danish death rates in the year 1980 for females and in the year 1990 for males. At the same time, areas with excess Danish mortality started to appear at age 50 for females and at age 70 for males. In the recent years, unfavorable trends continued, thus worsening the situation with excess Danish mortality. In the year 1999, higher Danish death rates are to be observed at ages from 40 to 80, in the case of females, and ages from 60 to 85, in the case of males. The differences in death rates between females are found to be more profound than the differences in the male populations.

At oldest-old ages (>80), Danish death rates have been lower than the Austrian up until the 1990s. Especially marked difference are to observed in the period from 1970 to 1990 in the female populations, when the Danish death rates were on average 30% lower. In the 1990s, the Danish advantage had mostly disappeared. Even if death rates in the female population of Denmark are still lower than in Austria, the excess of Austrian mortality is only about 10–20% and it appears only at ages 90 and above. For males, no statistically significant results have been obtained, except for ages 80–85, where Austrian death rates seem to be slightly lower than the Danish.

4.7 Denmark to France

The mortality surface of France has been estimated by Vallin, 1973. More recent data have been obtained from Institut national d'études démographiques, France (INED)[14]. In the present analysis, exposure and occurrences estimates, computed by J. Wilmoth for France,[15] whom utilized essentially the same data, have been used as well.

The relative differences in mortality of males shown in Figure 4.6 are obvious and easy to interpret. For over 80 years, the death rates in Denmark were considerably lower than in France (1899–1980). The excess of French mortality is apparent at all ages, except for childhood ages for the period after 1950. The results of estimating the ratio of death rates in this age group was not statistically significant, this is because death rates in both countries already fell to very low levels in the 1950s. In all other age groups, French males suffered from considerably higher death rates. Over the period 1899–1945, the French death rates for the population ages 20–59, were on average twice as high as in Denmark. At older ages

---

[14] www.ined.fr

[15] http://www.demog.berkeley.edu/wilmoth/mortality/

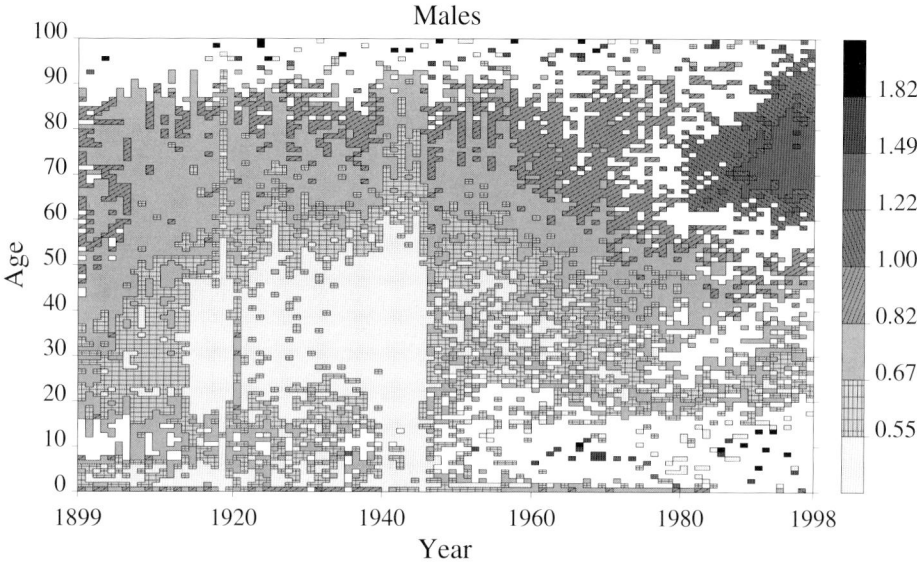

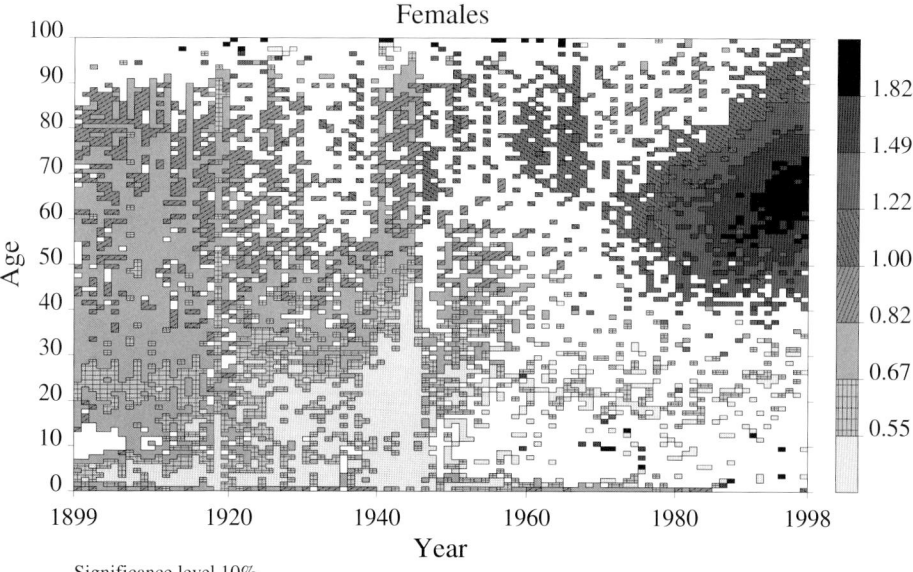

Significance level 10%

Figure 4.6. Ratio of death rates, Denmark to France

(>60), the excess of French mortality was about 30%.

Over time, the death rates in both countries converged and already by the year 1980, the first signs of higher Danish mortality at ages 65–75 came into view. Due to the rapid decline of the French mortality at older ages, a relative difference in death rates in this age group continued to grow until the recent years, simultaneously proliferating to older ages. In the year 1997, for example, higher Danish death rates are to be observed at all ages above 60, with the excess of mortality of 20–30%. At ages below 60, Danish death rates continued to be lower than those of France by an average of 30%.

When comparing females, we found a similar excess of French mortality up until the year 1945. French females suffered from higher mortality throughout all age ranges and especially for ages under 40. A similar phenomenon of convergence of death rates in both populations is also found between females, but it occurred much earlier than it did for the males. Already in the period 1950–1970, death rates in both countries were very close to each other. In the beginning of the 1970s, death rates in the female population of France fell below the levels of the Danish population and the area of excess Danish mortality started to emerge in the age group 50–60. Over time, unfavorable trends in Danish death rates continued to prevail in the mortality dynamics, redoubling the difference in death rates between two countries. It occurred in much the same manner as we found in the comparisons with other countries, e.g. Sweden or the Netherlands. In the year 1997, for example, Danish death rates at in the age group 60–70 were twice as high as their French counterparts.

4.8 Denmark to England and Wales

A series of death rates for England and Wales have been available since 1841. The mortality surface for England and Wales has been estimated by D. Philipov with significant support from Steve Smallwood. The data for ages 80 and above have been taken from the Kannisto-Thatcher database on old age mortality. Death counts classified by single year of age have been published in England and Wales only since the year 1911. For earlier years, data were available only by 5-year age groups and they were interpolated by single age using techniques similar to those used by Andreev in his work on the construction of the Danish mortality database (Andreev, 1999). Data for ages 85 and over during the period 1841–1910 were not available.

During the period 1841–1900, Danish death rates were significantly higher at ages 5 to 15 (Fig. 4.7). This finding is consistent with the results of the comparison with the populations of Sweden, Norway and the Netherlands. In all other age groups, Danish mortality was considerably lower. In the beginning of 20th century, the Danish mortality disadvantage at childhood ages virtually disappeared and death

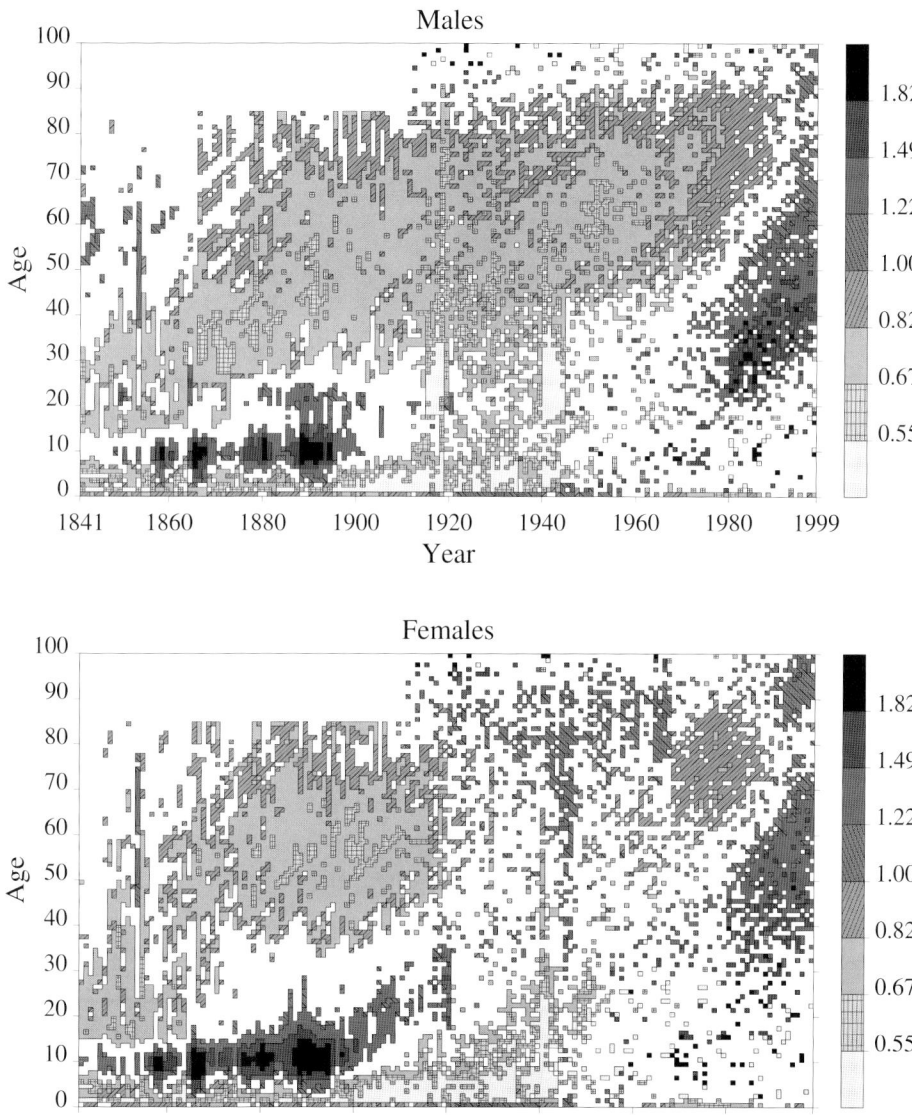

Significance level 10%

Figure 4.7. Ratio of death rates, Denmark to England and Wales

rates in the male population of England and Wales outnumbered the Danish death rates at practically all ages. Considerably lower Danish death rates in the female populations, prevailed at childhood ages (<15), while mortality of the higher ages in the two countries was nearly the same.

In the period after Second World War, death rates in the two countries were even more close to each other. The differences between the female populations were unimportant. The death rates of the portion of the population above age 80 in England and Wales, were slightly lower than that in Denmark, while in the age group 60–80 Danish females had the benefit of slightly lower mortality. As regards, males differences in death rates at age 40 and lower were also insignificant. At higher ages, however, English and Welsh death rates were still appreciably higher. For example, in the period from 1950 to 1980 and in the age group 40–80, death rates in England and Wales were on average 30% higher than in Denmark.

Starting with the 1980s, significant changes in the mortality regime between the two countries occurred. Stagnation of mortality in Denmark and the continuing decline of mortality in England and Wales, led to the emergence of excess Danish mortality at middle ages. The timing of emergence and dynamics over time bears a resemblance to the pattern found when comparing Danish and Dutch death rates. Such adverse developments in Danish death rates led to the excess of Danish mortality in the 1990s, amounting approximately to 30%.

It is also worth noting that the onset of emergence of female mortality lies somewhat later in time than compared with the findings from analysis on other countries. The first signs of a higher Danish mortality appeared only in the beginning of the 1980s, while the comparison with other countries points to the late 1960s as a likely point, when the problems with survival in the female population of Denmark started to manifest themselves.

4.9 Denmark to Japan

Data for Japan have been obtained from the BMD mortality database[16] and data for the recent years have been received directly from the National Statistical Office of Japan.

Death rates in Japan fell extremely rapid after the Second World War, placing this country among the longest-lived populations of nowadays. This rapid decline of Japanese mortality is clearly manifested in Fig. 4.8. During the period 1950–1970, the mortality in Denmark was much lower and the excess of Japanese mortality is to be observed virtually with all ages except for the oldest-old (>95). On average, death

---

[16] http://www.demog.berkeley.edu/wilmoth/mortality/

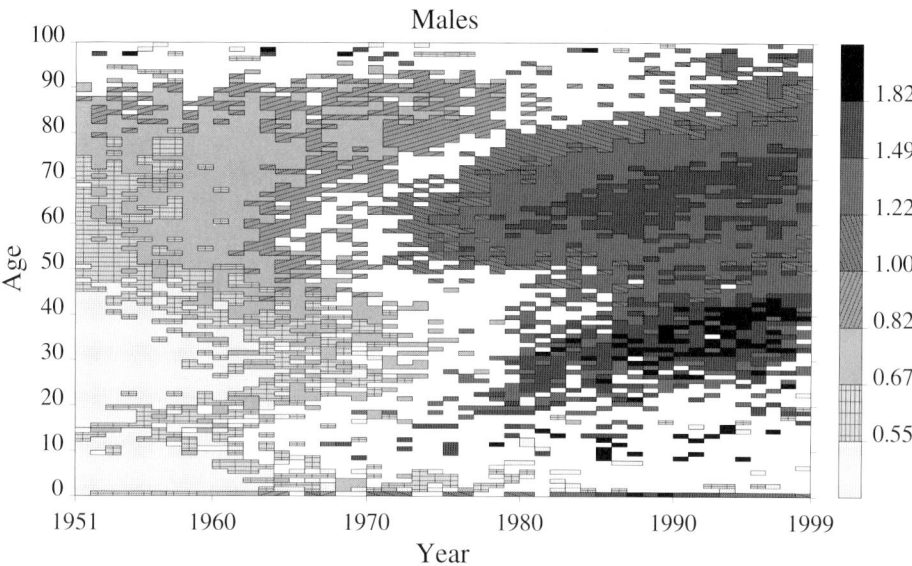

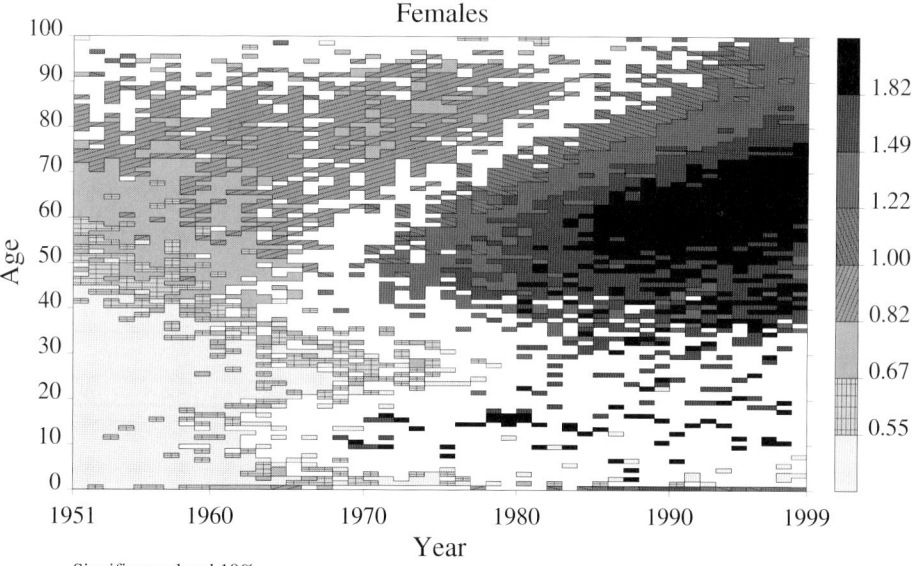

Significance level 10%

Figure 4.8. Ratio of death rates, Denmark to Japan

rates in Japan were about 60% higher than compared with that of Denmark.

Starting in the 1970s, the pattern completely reversed due to the rapid decline in Japanese mortality. In the case of the male populations, excess Danish mortality began to occur at age 60 in the earlier 1970s and it spread out to other ages over time. Concurrently, another area of abundant mortality began to occur at young ages. In the most recent years, the excess of Danish male mortality is apparent at all ages over 20, but especially in the age groups 65–80 and 30–40, where mortality differences are over 50%.

Comparing the female populations reveals even more profound differences between the two countries in the last three decades. Similar to males, an area with excess Danish mortality at ages 50–60 started to appear in the earlier 1970s. The excess of Danish mortality shown in Fig. 4.8 is the most drastic and the most extensive of all comparisons performed in this chapter. In 1998, death rates in Denmark were more than 90% higher at all ages in the range from 40 to 80, and about 110% higher in the age group 60–80. In contrast to males, there is no distinct mortality excess at young adult ages; Danish female death rates seem to be higher at ages 30–35, but the difference is less marked and often not statistically significant.

4.10 Denmark to Canada

The last country included in the comparison with the population of Denmark is Canada. Data for Canada are available since 1921 and they were provided by Thomas Burch and Statistics Canada. For ages above 80, the extinct population estimates from the Kannisto-Thatcher database on old age mortality have been also used.

Age specific differences in the survival between the two countries are clearly revealed in Fig. 4.9. The pattern of age-specific differences is very similar for males and females. Until 1980, the Danish death rates were generally lower at all ages below 65. In contrast, Canadian death rates were significantly lower at higher ages. The differences between males are more marked for lower ages, while for females, it is the youngest and the oldest ages where mortality between countries differs at most.

In the 1980s, the pattern radically changed. At childhood and young adult ages (<35), death rates in both countries converged to essentially the same levels. One exception is the male population in the age group 15–20, where Danish death rates are still significantly lower. Canadian death rates above age 35, declined to levels lower than the Danish death rates, producing an excess of Danish mortality of virtually all ages for the years 1980 and onwards. Generally Danish death rates were about 25% higher for males and 35% higher for females during the period 1980–

81

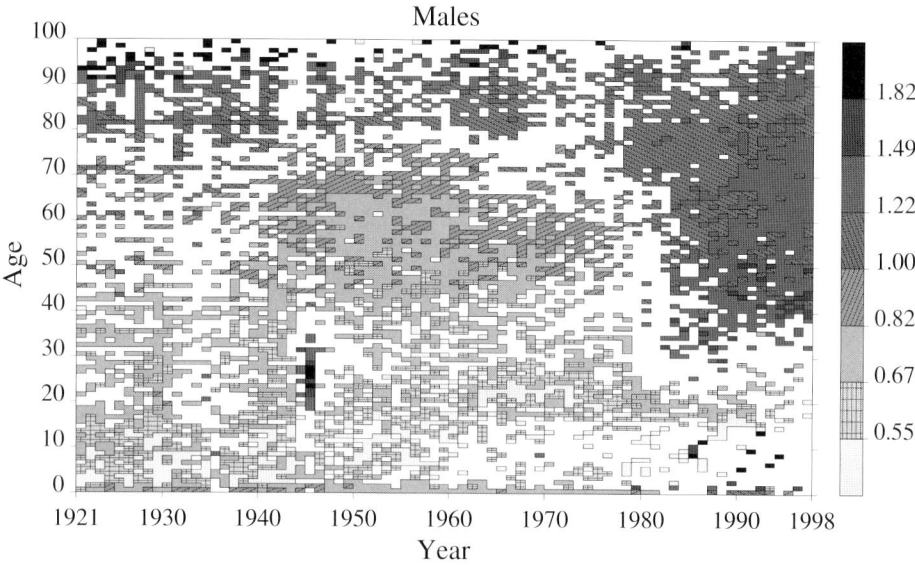

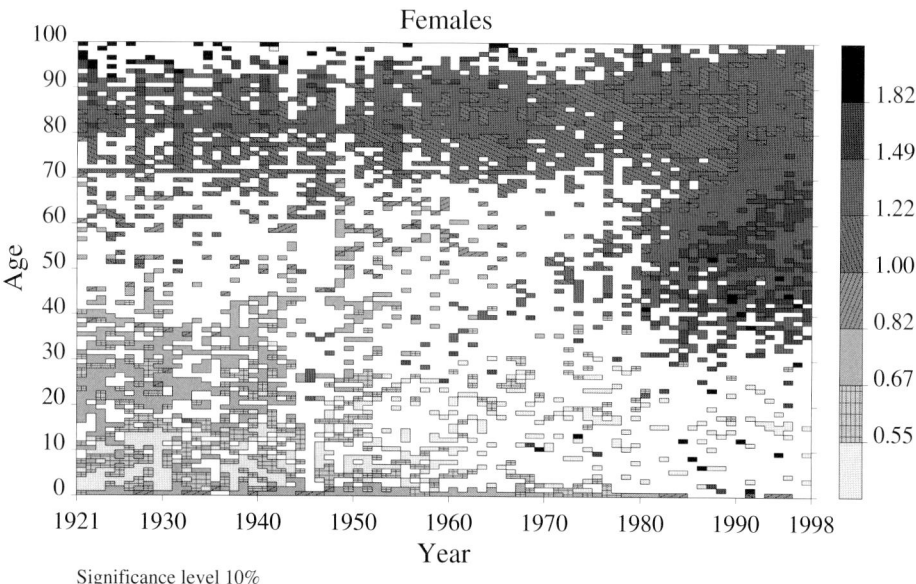

Significance level 10%

Figure 4.9. Ratio of death rates, Denmark to Canada

1997 and at ages 35 and above.

A distinct feature of Fig. 4.9, which is not found in any of the other comparisons, is the excess of Danish mortality at the oldest-old ages (80 and over). The previous analysis indicates that Danish death rates at such advanced ages were not exceptionally high when compared with the other countries. Moreover, in many cases they were considerably lower. Thus the results presented in Fig. 4.9 are attributed to the exceptionally low mortality in Canada, rather than to the notably high oldest-old mortality in Denmark. Why the oldest-old mortality in Canada is remarkably low is a further subject of ongoing demographic research.

4.11 Concluding notes

Reconstruction of time series of death rates over long periods of time inevitably raises questions about data quality and data comparability. Estimates of infant mortality rates, death rates at the highest ages and death rates in earlier periods are especially prone to contain errors. Problems with infant death rates arise mostly from different definitions of infants deaths adopted in different countries. Over time, such definitions might be revised producing artificial changes in trends in infant mortality rates. Making necessary adjustments for obtaining a comparable series of infant death rates can be a non-trivial task (Tabeau et. al., 1994; Vallin, 1973). Thus results for infant mortality have to be taken cautiously.

As regards data for earlier periods, they are commonly less detailed, which entails an additional adjustment of data for the estimation of mortality surfaces. In the 19th century, for example, data on deaths for Denmark and England and Wales had to be distributed by single year of age from original data aggregated into 5-year age groups. Populations between censuses had to be estimated indirectly, e. g. by the method of balance equation, and if the census population were given by 5-year age groups, it required an additional estimation of single-age population structure. Quality of mortality estimates for such periods will be necessarily poorer, if the estimates were based on deaths available by single year of age, but general patterns of mortality differences between countries will be nevertheless captured satisfactory.

At older ages, poor quality of data stems from age misreporting in censuses and in death registration statistics. Such errors in the data usually lead to the implausibly low estimates of death rates at advanced ages and unreasonable trends in death rates over time. The extinct cohort method usually produces more reliable population estimates at advanced ages, so it was employed whenever possible for the estimation of death rates at ages 80 and over. One current research question presently under investigation, is to find out whether the Canadian advantage of low oldest-old mortality (Fig. 4.9) is an artifact of bad quality data.

Certain problems also arise from different classification schemes adopted by the National Statistical Offices. For example, deaths could be classified either by single year and age, as in England and Wales, or by single year of birth and age, as in the case of Norway. Distributing deaths by Lexis triangles introduces an additional bias in mortality estimates.

Despite all the problems with the reconstruction of mortality trends over extended periods of time, the results presented in this chapter can be considered reliable. Before the analysis, all raw data were scrutinized and subjected to various quality checks. Only data, which appeared to be reasonable, were included in the present analysis. In addition, all of the countries selected for the analysis have a long tradition of collecting population and vital statistics and are consequently considered reliable by the demographic community. Altogether, it allows us to make the following conclusions.

First, I would like to note that the analysis presented in this chapter, helped us to look at the mortality developments in Denmark for more than 150 years and from an international perspective. An examination revealed some remarkable features in the Danish mortality evaluation. In the second half of 19th century, the mortality transition in Denmark was among the mainstream of European countries. Danish death rates were somewhat higher than those in Sweden and Norway, but lower than the death rates in the Netherlands and England and Wales. One exception from this pattern, is the age group 5–15, where the death rates in Denmark for both sexes were significantly higher than in other countries. By the end of the 19th century, the Danish mortality disadvantage in this age group, however, appears to sharply diminish and disappear.

In the first half of the 20th century, mortality conditions in Denmark were quite favorable. The rapid mortality decline secured a place for Denmark among the longest-lived countries. Danish mortality advantage at childhood, young and young adult ages (<60) were so obvious during the first decades of the 20th century, that Danish life expectancy at birth was perhaps the highest among European countries. This is consistent with findings presented by Vallin (Table 3.2). There is some evidence, however, that the Danish female death rates at adult ages were slightly higher than those in other countries. Nevertheless this disadvantage cannot significantly influence the estimates of the life expectancy at birth, because the death rates at younger ages were still rather high and their influence on estimates of life expectancy at birth was the highest among all ages.

In the second half of the 20th century, the Danish mortality advantage to a large extent disappeared, which resulted in the emergence of areas with abundant

Danish mortality at the middle ages. Particular unfavorable developments were found in the population of females, where death rates started to lag behind those in other developed countries by the 1970s. For males, a similar phenomenon is to be observed as well, but it is less outstanding and it came only into view during the 1980s. Due to the unfavorable trends in Danish mortality, female death rates appeared to be the highest among all countries in the last several years at ages 40–80 and male death rates at ages 60–80.

Figures 4.10 and 4.11 make it easier to comprehend the results summarized in this section. Fig. 4.10 shows years and ages where death rates in Denmark were the highest among all countries for which data were available in the given period. Fig. 4.11, shows years and ages where the death rates were the lowest. Excess of female mortality in the period 1970–1999 (Fig. 4.10) and Danish mortality advantage in the period 1900–1950 (Fig. 4.11) appear especially eye-catching.

The Danish mortality disadvantage in the recent years is a notable phenomenon and it definitely calls for explanation. One way to gain a deeper understanding about the factors behind the excess of Danish mortality is to examine the trends in cause-specific mortality. For obvious reasons, data on the causes of death are less reliable and less detailed than those analyzed here, but we are now concerned with statistics for recent decades, where data quality should be reasonably good to draw some useful conclusions. This is subject of the following chapter.

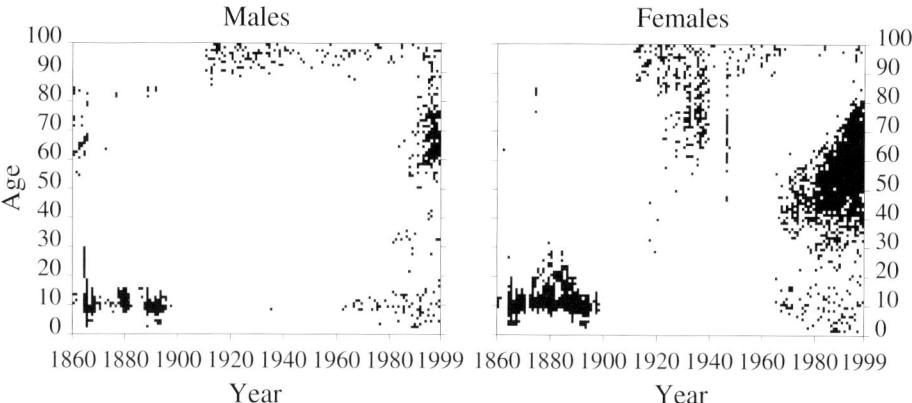

Figure 4.10. The highest death rates in Denmark compared with other countries

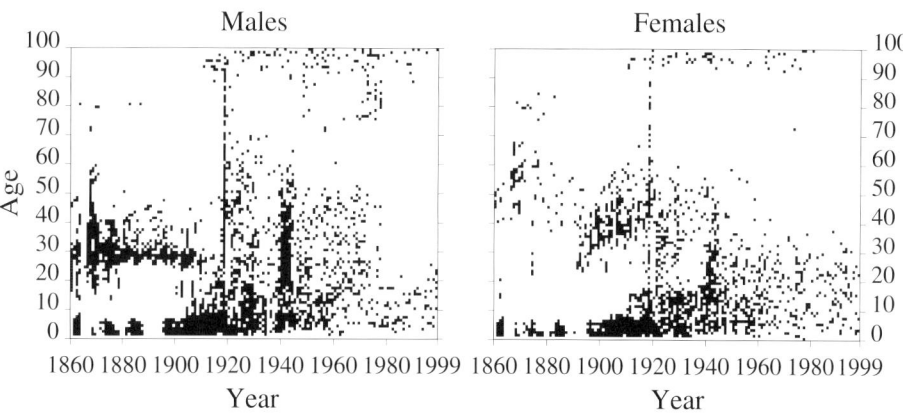

Figure 4.11. The lowest death rates in Denmark compared with other countries

5. Cause-specific mortality

5.1 An analysis of cause-specific mortality

One of the main findings, described in the previous chapter, is the unusual excess of Danish mortality in recent years. This phenomenon can be investigated in different ways. An analysis of the causes of death is one of the most important directions for further research. For my comparison, I have selected three countries: Sweden, the Netherlands and Japan. Sweden is chosen to represent the experience of the Nordic countries and the Netherlands is to represent the central part of Europe. Japan is interesting, since differences between Danish and Japanese death rates are now the highest, when compared to the other countries.

The mortality database maintained by the World Health Organization (WHO) includes death counts classified by causes of death for all countries throughout the world. Utilizing such data makes it possible for us to analyze cause-specific mortality differences between countries. These data have been used extensively in studies devoted to the stagnation of Danish life expectancy (Sundhedsministeriets Middellevetidsudvalg, 1993; Bjerregaard and Juel, 1993; Bjerregaard and Juel, 1994). The analysis presented in this section has two main objectives. The first goal is to decompose excess Danish mortality by causes of deaths, in order to reveal the causes of death contributing most to the excess of Danish mortality. The second is to survey the trends in cause-specific death rates.

For this purpose, I have downloaded the mortality data from the WHO web site[17] and extracted the relevant country-specific data from the raw mortality files. Then, I created an abridged list of 25 causes of deaths (Appendix Table 8) and aggregated the death counts using this custom classification. The causes of deaths included in the abridged list, were selected after a careful examination of scientific publications related to the current analysis.

The method of excess mortality decomposition that I used here is very simple, and the interpretation of the results is based on the assumption of the independence of causes of death. The relative excess mortality for a given period and in a certain age group can be computed as

$$\rho = \left(\frac{m}{m'} - 1\right) \cdot 100\% \qquad (5.1)$$

where m and m' are the central death rates (cf. e.g. Chiang, 1984) in Denmark and the country selected for comparison, respectively. The ratio of death rates is then:

---

[17] www.who.int/whosis/mort/

$$\frac{m}{m'} = \frac{\sum_i m_i}{\sum_i m'_i} = 1 + \frac{\sum_i \Delta_i}{\sum_i m'_i} \qquad (5.2)$$

where m_i is the mortality rate from the ith cause of death and $\Delta_i = m_i - m'_i$ is the absolute difference in mortality from the ith cause of death in Denmark and another country. Finally,

$$\rho = \sum_i \rho_i \qquad (5.3)$$

where $\rho_i = \frac{\Delta_i}{\sum_i m'_i} \cdot 100\%$ is the contribution of the ith cause of death in the total excess mortality.

As can be seen in Fig. 4.10, the most striking differences in mortality are observed at ages 50–70, and this pattern has remained more or less stable since 1970. Following this observation, I applied this method to decompose the mortality differences in Denmark and other countries for the period 1985–1993, for 4 age groups: 50–54, 55–59, 60–64 and 65–69. Table 5.1 shows the computed values of ρ_i by cause of death, age group, sex, and country. The last row of the table shows the total excess mortality (equation 5.1). For example, female death rates in Denmark in the period 1985–1993 for ages 60–64 were on average 58.62% higher than in Sweden (Table 5.1). The 9.65% out of 58.62% are attributed to lung cancer (cause 2; Malignant neoplasm of trachea, bronchus and lungs; Appendix Table 8); 5.28% to breast cancer (cause 7) etc. Positive values of ρ_i, which indicate a significant contribution to excess mortality (>2%), have been highlighted to facilitate the reading of this table. I must also note that two sets of estimates of excess mortality, (based on WHO data and on the data published by the national statistical offices) are in agreement for all populations, but the Netherlands. For the male and female populations of the Netherlands, excess Danish mortality is somewhat higher if it is estimated from the WHO data.

Table 5.1 contains a great deal of material, which the interested reader will wish to examine for him or herself. Here a few general comments:

a) **Denmark vs. Sweden, Males.** The main contribution to excess Danish mortality stems from the higher mortality from lung cancer (cause 2). Approximately 25% of the overall excess mortality can be attributed to this case of death. Higher mortality from the residual group of neoplasm (8) is also apparent in all age groups, but its contribution is less substantial and it decreases with age. In the lower age groups (50–64), mortality from ischaemic heart disease (9), cirrhosis of the liver (18) and suicide (21) is also significantly higher in Denmark. At ages 65–69, contribution of these causes of deaths to the total mortality excess is, however, quite small. On the contrary, excess mortality from respiratory diseases (15) increases sharply with age. At ages 60–69, it accounts for about 15% of the total excess.

b) **Denmark vs the Netherlands, Males.** The two most important causes of death with higher Danish mortality are the residual neoplasm group (8) and ischaemic heart disease (9). The latter accounts for about 20% of the total excess mortality at ages 50–54 and 45% at ages 64–69; the residual neoplasm group makes up approximately 15% of the excess mortality. In contrast to comparisons with other populations, mortality from lung cancer is actually lower in Denmark than in the Netherlands. This finding is rather surprising, since a higher mortality from lung cancer in Denmark has been observed in all other comparisons - for both the male and female populations. In the age group 50–54, where excess Danish mortality was the highest, significant differences are to be seen in death rates from cirrhosis of the liver (18) and as well suicide (21). The contribution of these causes of death to excess mortality declines with age and becomes negligible in higher age groups.

c) **Denmark vs Japan, Males.** In this comparison, the analysis reveals striking differences in the mortality from ischaemic heart disease (9), which is responsible for about 70% of the excess Danish mortality. The next important cause of death is lung cancer (2), which is also appreciably higher in Denmark than in Japan. The third important cause contributing to excess mortality is disease of the respiratory system (15).

d) **Denmark vs Sweden, Females.** The highest mortality differences exist in the area of cancer, especially lung cancer (2), residual cancers (8) and breast cancer (7). Altogether, these 3 causes of death account for about 40% of the observed excess mortality. Other important contributors to excess Danish mortality are respiratory diseases (15) and ischaemic heart disease (9). The contribution to excess mortality from the group 'Bronchitis, emphysema and asthma' (15) is noticeably higher than from ischaemic heart disease (9), and it is as important as lung cancer, at ages 65–69. At ages 50–59, we can also see the marked differences in death rates from cirrhosis of the liver (18) and suicide (21). At higher ages, mortality differences from these causes of death are less pronounced. An excess of mortality from cerebrovascular disease (11) is also noticeable, although its contribution seems to be less significant than from the causes mentioned above.

Table 5.1 Decomposition of excess Danish mortality by causes of death for the period 1985–1993. Males.

The table shows the contribution of a particular cause of death to the total excess mortality (%). A description of the causes of death together with the WHO category numbers is provided in Appendix Table 8. Causes of death contributing more than 2% to excess mortality appear in boldface type.

Cause	Sweden				Netherlands				Japan			
Ages	50–54	55–59	60–64	65–69	50–54	55–59	60–64	65–69	50–54	55–59	60–64	65–69
1	1.12	0.47	0.11	-0.12	1.25	0.69	0.11	-0.05	-0.08	-0.70	-1.15	-1.50
2	**5.86**	**8.49**	**9.48**	**8.87**	-1.46	-0.89	-1.10	-1.71	**7.11**	**9.96**	**10.11**	**9.27**
3	0.02	0.13	-0.23	-0.34	0.40	0.78	0.71	1.25	0.79	1.66	**2.52**	**3.94**
4	0.27	0.78	1.04	1.11	-0.23	0.45	0.57	0.31	0.06	0.65	1.14	1.40
5	0.50	0.15	0.01	-0.30	-0.25	-0.65	-0.82	-0.79	-6.63	-7.50	-7.98	-7.80
6	0.52	0.87	0.82	1.11	0.64	1.18	1.12	1.31	-0.27	0.20	0.38	1.12
7	0.09	0.08	0.07	0.05	0.09	0.09	0.07	0.05	0.09	0.09	0.08	0.06
8	**6.71**	**5.18**	**5.03**	**3.82**	**5.53**	**4.52**	**4.22**	**3.05**	**2.57**	-0.87	0.47	**2.32**
9	**4.70**	**4.17**	**2.16**	0.62	**8.18**	**10.56**	**10.34**	**10.76**	**26.12**	**32.27**	**36.63**	**38.95**
10	-0.70	-0.55	0.01	-0.28	-2.43	-2.32	-2.13	-2.72	-6.10	-5.15	-4.48	-4.98
11	1.31	0.58	0.95	0.88	1.95	1.66	1.80	1.52	-6.11	-4.91	-3.37	-2.67
12	0.58	0.17	0.77	0.42	0.76	0.13	0.33	-0.04	1.35	1.49	**2.77**	**3.35**
13	0.86	1.15	1.21	1.14	0.98	1.25	1.45	1.37	1.03	1.47	1.92	**2.04**
14	-1.36	-1.05	-0.74	-0.70	0.22	0.38	0.38	0.35	-1.25	-1.58	-2.52	-3.92
15	1.40	**3.02**	**4.47**	**5.30**	1.42	**2.41**	**2.51**	**2.18**	2.00	**3.99**	**6.04**	**7.49**
16	0.01	0.01	0.06	0.01	-0.02	0.01	0.03	0.00	0.02	0.03	0.08	0.06
17	0.39	0.10	0.18	0.26	0.37	0.19	0.29	0.19	-0.29	-0.64	-0.80	-1.12
18	**4.67**	**2.89**	1.63	1.03	**5.96**	**4.25**	**2.39**	1.26	-0.12	-0.59	-0.44	-0.26
19	-0.10	-0.03	0.19	0.18	0.42	0.39	0.44	0.45	0.13	0.15	0.38	0.47
20	-0.58	-0.05	0.06	0.09	-0.01	0.12	-0.11	-0.19	-0.84	-0.52	-0.48	-0.29
21	**3.16**	1.54	1.42	0.70	**7.10**	**3.50**	**2.26**	1.23	1.87	0.88	1.32	0.75
22	1.10	0.35	0.44	0.28	1.09	0.49	0.51	0.25	-0.16	-0.54	-0.19	-0.27
23	-0.17	-0.25	-0.02	0.11	0.55	0.31	0.40	0.32	-0.14	-0.19	0.12	0.26
24	-2.91	-1.87	-1.49	-0.71	**2.68**	1.48	0.62	0.31	-0.35	-0.64	-0.97	-0.96
25	**9.88**	**9.34**	**7.97**	**6.44**	**8.95**	**6.85**	**4.80**	**2.96**	**14.56**	**12.67**	**10.61**	**8.86**
Total	37.35	35.66	35.60	29.98	44.15	37.85	31.19	23.63	35.34	41.69	52.19	56.59

Table 5.1 (cont.) Females.

Cause	Sweden				Netherlands				Japan			
Ages	50–54	55–59	60–64	65–69	50–54	55–59	60–64	65–69	50–54	55–59	60–64	65–69
1	0.26	0.28	0.04	-0.10	0.30	0.43	0.22	0.13	-0.47	-0.49	-0.85	-0.77
2	8.58	12.58	9.65	7.15	9.21	12.63	10.24	9.15	14.04	19.31	15.27	10.80
3	0.00	0.00	0.00	0.00	0.00	0.00	0.00	0.00	0.00	0.00	0.00	0.00
4	1.65	2.19	1.84	1.34	1.19	1.89	1.37	0.78	2.32	3.51	3.23	2.83
5	-0.20	0.42	-0.23	-0.54	0.12	0.73	-0.04	-0.35	-7.28	-5.82	-5.94	-5.49
6	0.78	0.92	1.11	0.84	1.20	1.46	1.74	1.52	0.34	0.93	1.48	1.28
7	9.14	7.77	5.28	3.72	4.41	4.37	2.35	1.72	19.81	18.98	14.47	10.47
8	8.52	9.23	8.63	4.50	13.31	14.28	13.74	9.80	20.19	23.97	22.22	16.50
9	4.08	5.60	5.45	3.57	4.13	6.54	9.57	10.50	11.92	18.71	25.07	27.32
10	-0.37	-0.59	0.17	-0.17	-1.57	-1.89	-1.45	-2.48	-4.97	-5.00	-4.72	-6.19
11	2.84	2.45	1.94	1.69	3.00	2.64	3.17	2.75	-3.47	-2.96	-2.15	-2.43
12	1.15	0.78	0.96	1.06	1.39	1.20	1.47	1.90	1.81	1.96	2.50	3.16
13	1.44	1.68	1.66	1.44	1.65	1.61	1.73	1.95	1.87	2.25	2.44	2.56
14	-0.08	-0.19	-0.41	-0.39	0.58	0.60	0.55	0.69	-0.48	-0.95	-1.41	-2.24
15	4.70	7.04	7.78	6.85	5.06	7.63	8.60	7.62	7.05	11.04	12.74	11.00
16	0.04	0.12	0.07	0.08	0.03	0.07	0.02	0.06	0.05	0.17	0.12	0.13
17	0.15	0.30	0.20	0.05	0.15	0.45	0.39	0.26	-0.38	-0.16	-0.34	-0.59
18	3.61	2.23	1.54	0.69	4.34	2.97	2.12	0.98	4.02	1.85	0.54	-0.70
19	0.61	0.66	0.73	0.67	0.95	0.86	1.01	1.05	1.00	1.05	1.22	1.17
20	0.12	0.47	0.44	0.39	0.27	0.44	0.27	0.13	0.40	0.57	0.68	0.40
21	6.14	3.97	2.63	1.55	8.33	5.09	3.05	1.98	6.98	4.51	2.51	1.01
22	0.56	0.12	0.19	0.31	0.88	0.40	0.27	0.22	0.25	-0.16	-0.18	-0.13
23	0.20	0.34	0.48	0.43	0.24	0.27	0.52	0.70	0.38	0.53	0.85	1.03
24	1.27	0.00	-0.31	-0.07	4.27	1.95	1.07	0.58	3.74	1.34	0.32	-0.28
25	9.67	10.68	8.76	8.45	8.91	7.79	5.41	4.29	15.36	15.87	13.29	11.91
Total	64.86	69.05	58.62	43.52	72.37	74.39	67.41	55.95	94.48	111.02	103.35	82.75

e) **Denmark vs the Netherlands, Females.** The general structure of the cause-specific excess mortality is quite similar to that found when comparing Danish and Swedish data. However, mortality differences in ischaemic heart disease (9) at high ages and the differences in suicide (21) mortality in the lower age groups are higher than those found in the comparison to Sweden.

f) **Denmark vs Japan, Females.** Similar to the comparisons with Sweden and Denmark, the analysis indicates that the following causes of deaths are the most significant contributors to excess of Danish mortality: lung cancer (2), breast cancer (7), residual malignant neoplasm (8), ischaemic heart disease (9), and respiratory diseases (15). In addition, at ages 50–59, a substantial contribution is also provided by the differences in mortality from cirrhosis of the liver (18) and suicide (21).

The residual group of diseases (25) includes the remaining causes of death, which have not been classified in any of the other 24 categories (Appendix Table 8). As can be seen in Table 5.1, these residual causes of death also provide an appreciable contribution to excess Danish mortality for all countries and for all age groups. The relative importance of the causes of death in a group (25) reflects, above all, the fact that different diagnostic and coding practices have been adopted in the different countries. In the case of Denmark, there is a relatively high proportion of deaths that are classified as unknown or ill-defined cases.

If precise diagnostics were possible, one might expect that the absolute contributions to excess Danish mortality from the specific causes of deaths would be even higher, since more deaths would be allocated to the specific disease categories. However, the relative contribution of a particular cause of death to excess Danish mortality in this case, might thereby change.

In sum, the results presented in Table 5.1 should be considered suggestive, but not conclusive. The problem we are facing here is rooted in the quality of data on cause-specific mortality. In addition to the large group of residual diseases, the results related to the diseases of the circulatory and the respiratory systems (Appendix Table 7, chapters III and IV) should be viewed with greater caution than others (Juel and Sjol, 1995; Bjerregaard and Juel, 1993).

Yet another source of errors is the different classifications of diseases used by countries submitting data to the WHO. This sometimes makes it difficult to restore time trends of specific causes of deaths. Denmark used the 8th revision of the International Classification of Disease (ICD) from 1969 to 1993, while in the Netherlands and Japan, this classification was used only up until 1979 and in Sweden until 1987. After these dates, death counts were reported in these countries using the 9th revision of the ICD. In contrast, Denmark never made of use the 9th revision of the ICD, but has used the 10th revision since 1994. Here is one example of the problems associated with the transition from the 8th to the 9th revision: in Japan, this resulted in an abrupt jump in death rates from the 10th cause of death (other forms of heart disease); a similar jump is also noticeable in the Netherlands, but not in Sweden.

To minimize the effect of problems associated with misclassification and to improve the overall quality of results, I aggregated the causes of deaths by disease *categories* included in the chapters of Appendix Table 8. By aggregating the data, it is possible to obtain more reliable results, but the structure of those causes of death that provide contributions to excess Danish mortality will be less detailed. I repeated the procedure described above, using these broader categories of diseases. In addition, I computed the *relative* contribution of a particular cause of death to excess Danish mortality and included it in Table 5.2. The highlighted items in Table 5.2 are the causes of death that provide the highest contribution to the excess Danish mortality.

As is evident from Table 5.2, there are striking similarities among the results for the female populations. In all countries and at all ages, excess mortality from cancer (group II) has made the highest contribution to the observed mortality differences. The numbers range from 40 to 50% of total excess mortality. Cardiovascular diseases (III) and respiratory diseases (IV) take second and third place, respectively, in order of importance. At ages 50–54, however, the most important contribution (after cancer) comes from mortality from accidents, poisonings, and violence (VI), leaving the cardiovascular and respiratory diseases behind.

The results obtained for male populations are less homogeneous between the countries. However, in the case of Sweden, the pattern is similar to that observed in the female populations, i.e., the main contribution is attributed to cancer mortality followed by cardiovascular mortality and mortality from respiratory diseases. Generally, about 45% of excess mortality is related to cancer. We also note that the importance of respiratory diseases rises significantly with age and that this is the age group 65–69, where mortality differences are more pronounced. In addition, at ages 50–54 the group of digestive diseases, including cirrhosis of the liver, constitutes a significant part of excess mortality.

As follows from Table 5.2, the male population of Japan has a striking advantage of lower mortality from cardiovascular diseases. The differences in death rates from cancer, also provide a positive contribution to excess Danish mortality, but this is less marked. Approximately 60% of the excess mortality (Denmark vs. Japan) can be attributed to cardiovascular diseases, 15% to malignant neoplasms and about 4% to respiratory diseases. The Japanese levels of mortality from other causes of death are comparable with the Danish levels.

Compared to the male population of the Netherlands, the most notable mortality differences are to be observed in cardiovascular mortality (III). Death rates from this cause of death account for 30% of the total mortality differences at ages 55–59 and about 45% at ages 65–69. However, at ages 50–54, the highest contribution did not come from the cardiovascular diseases, but from accidents (VI), which accounted for 25% of the total excess mortality. With advancing age, the importance of accidents falls, while contribution of cancers (II) and diseases of respiratory system (IV) increases. Altogether, these causes of death account for 26% of the total mortality excess at ages 65–69.

5.2   Time trends in cause-specific mortality

The analysis presented in the previous section helped us to highlight the most important causes of death contributing to excess Danish mortality in middle age. Another question of principal interest involves trends in death rates from specific causes of death. I have computed the series of death rates for the period from 1970 to 1993 by 4 age groups for all countries included in the analysis. The year 1970 was

Table 5.2 Decomposition of excess Danish mortality by aggregated causes of death for the period 1985–1993. Males.

The table shows both the absolute and relative contribution (%) of a particular group of diseases to the total excess mortality. A description of causes of death included in a particular group of diseases is provided in Appendix Table 8. The items in boldface are causes of death providing maximal contributions to excess mortality.

Chapter	Sweden				Netherlands				Japan			
Ages	50–54	55–59	60–64	65–69	50–54	55–59	60–64	65–69	50–54	55–59	60–64	65–69
	\multicolumn{12}{c}{Absolute contribution to excess mortality(%)}											
I	1.12	0.47	0.11	-0.12	1.25	0.69	0.11	-0.05	-0.08	-0.70	-1.15	-1.50
II	**13.97**	**15.68**	**16.22**	**14.31**	4.73	5.48	4.77	3.47	3.70	4.19	6.72	10.32
III	6.75	5.52	5.11	2.78	9.44	**11.29**	**11.79**	**10.88**	**16.28**	**25.17**	**33.47**	**36.69**
IV	0.44	2.08	3.97	4.88	2.00	2.99	3.21	2.72	0.48	1.80	2.79	2.51
V	4.00	2.81	1.88	1.31	6.37	4.77	2.72	1.53	-0.82	-0.96	-0.54	-0.07
VI	1.19	-0.24	0.34	0.37	**11.42**	5.78	3.80	2.11	1.22	-0.48	0.29	-0.22
VII	9.88	9.34	7.97	6.44	8.95	6.85	4.80	2.96	14.56	12.67	10.61	8.86
Total	37.35	35.66	35.60	29.98	44.15	37.85	31.19	23.63	35.34	41.69	52.19	56.59
	\multicolumn{12}{c}{Relative contribution to excess mortality (%)}											
I	2.99	1.33	0.31	-0.40	2.83	1.83	0.34	-0.20	-0.23	-1.68	-2.21	-2.65
II	**37.40**	**43.98**	**45.55**	**47.75**	10.71	14.48	15.28	14.70	10.48	10.04	12.88	18.23
III	18.08	15.47	14.34	9.28	21.38	**29.82**	**37.79**	**46.06**	**46.07**	**60.37**	**64.14**	**64.84**
IV	1.17	5.83	11.14	16.27	4.53	7.91	10.30	11.53	1.35	4.33	5.35	4.44
V	10.71	7.87	5.29	4.36	14.43	12.59	8.71	6.46	-2.33	-2.30	-1.04	-0.13
VI	3.18	-0.67	0.97	1.25	**25.86**	15.27	12.18	8.93	3.46	-1.15	0.56	-0.38
VII	26.46	26.19	22.40	21.49	20.26	18.09	15.40	12.52	41.19	30.38	20.33	15.66
Total	100.00	100.00	100.00	100.00	100.00	100.00	100.00	100.00	100.00	100.00	100.00	100.00

Table 5.2 (cont.) Females.

Chapter	Sweden				Netherlands				Japan			
Ages	50–54	55–59	60–64	65–69	50–54	55–59	60–64	65–69	50–54	55–59	60–64	65–69
Absolute contribution to excess mortality(%)												
I	0.26	0.28	0.04	-0.10	0.30	0.43	0.22	0.13	-0.47	-0.49	-0.85	-0.77
II	**28.47**	**33.11**	**26.28**	**17.00**	29.44	35.35	29.41	22.63	49.42	60.88	50.73	36.38
III	9.14	9.92	10.19	7.59	8.60	10.10	14.50	14.61	7.16	14.96	23.13	24.42
IV	4.80	7.26	7.64	6.59	5.83	8.74	9.57	8.64	6.24	10.10	11.11	8.30
V	4.35	3.36	2.71	1.76	5.57	4.27	3.40	2.17	5.41	3.48	2.45	0.87
VI	8.17	4.43	2.99	2.22	13.72	7.71	4.92	3.49	11.35	6.22	3.50	1.63
VII	9.67	10.68	8.76	8.45	8.91	7.79	5.41	4.29	15.36	15.87	13.29	11.91
Total	64.86	69.05	58.62	43.52	72.37	74.39	67.41	55.95	94.48	111.0	103.35	82.75
Relative contribution to excess mortality (%)												
I	0.40	0.41	0.07	-0.23	0.41	0.58	0.32	0.24	-0.50	-0.44	-0.82	-0.94
II	**43.90**	**47.95**	**44.84**	**39.06**	40.68	47.53	43.62	40.44	52.31	54.84	49.08	43.97
III	14.10	14.36	17.39	17.44	11.88	13.57	21.50	26.12	7.58	13.47	22.38	29.51
IV	7.40	10.52	13.03	15.15	8.06	11.75	14.19	15.44	6.61	9.10	10.75	10.03
V	6.70	4.87	4.63	4.05	7.70	5.74	5.05	3.87	5.73	3.13	2.37	1.05
VI	12.60	6.42	5.10	5.11	18.96	10.37	7.29	6.23	12.01	5.60	3.39	1.97
VII	14.90	15.47	14.94	19.42	12.31	10.47	8.02	7.66	16.26	14.30	12.86	14.40
Total	100.0	100.0	100.0	100.0	100.0	100.0	100.0	100.00	100.0	100.0	100.00	100.0

chosen, because it marks the emergence of the area of excess mortality, as can be seen in Fig. 4.10. In addition, all countries used the 8th revision of the ICD at that time, which permits us to avoid certain classification problems in the earlier years. Altogether, 200 plots[18] have been analyzed and 44 of them displaying the *disadvantageous* trends in Danish mortality are presented in Fig. 5.1(a,b). It must be emphasized, that the causes of deaths discussed below have been selected in order to shed light on Danish excess mortality. In other words, only causes of death, where Danish mortality is higher, are discussed here. The reader interested in the trends of all causes of death can explore the graphs provided on the CD-ROM for him or herself.

Male mortality from lung cancer (2) has been steadily increasing in Denmark, Sweden and Japan (except ages 50–54), but not in the Netherlands, here a moderate decline in mortality can be observed (Fig. 5.1(a)). During the whole period, Danish mortality has been double that of Sweden and Japan, but appreciably lower than that of the Netherlands. The decline in Dutch mortality led to the convergence of

---

[18] The plots with the trends in cause-specific mortality are provided on the accompanying CD-ROM. The files are stored in HTML format and can be viewed with any Web browser. If your CD-ROM drive is assigned the D: letter, open D:\CAUSES\CAUSE.HTM to start browsing.

Malignant neoplasm of the trachea, bronchus and lungs(2). Males

Ischaemic heart disease(9). Males

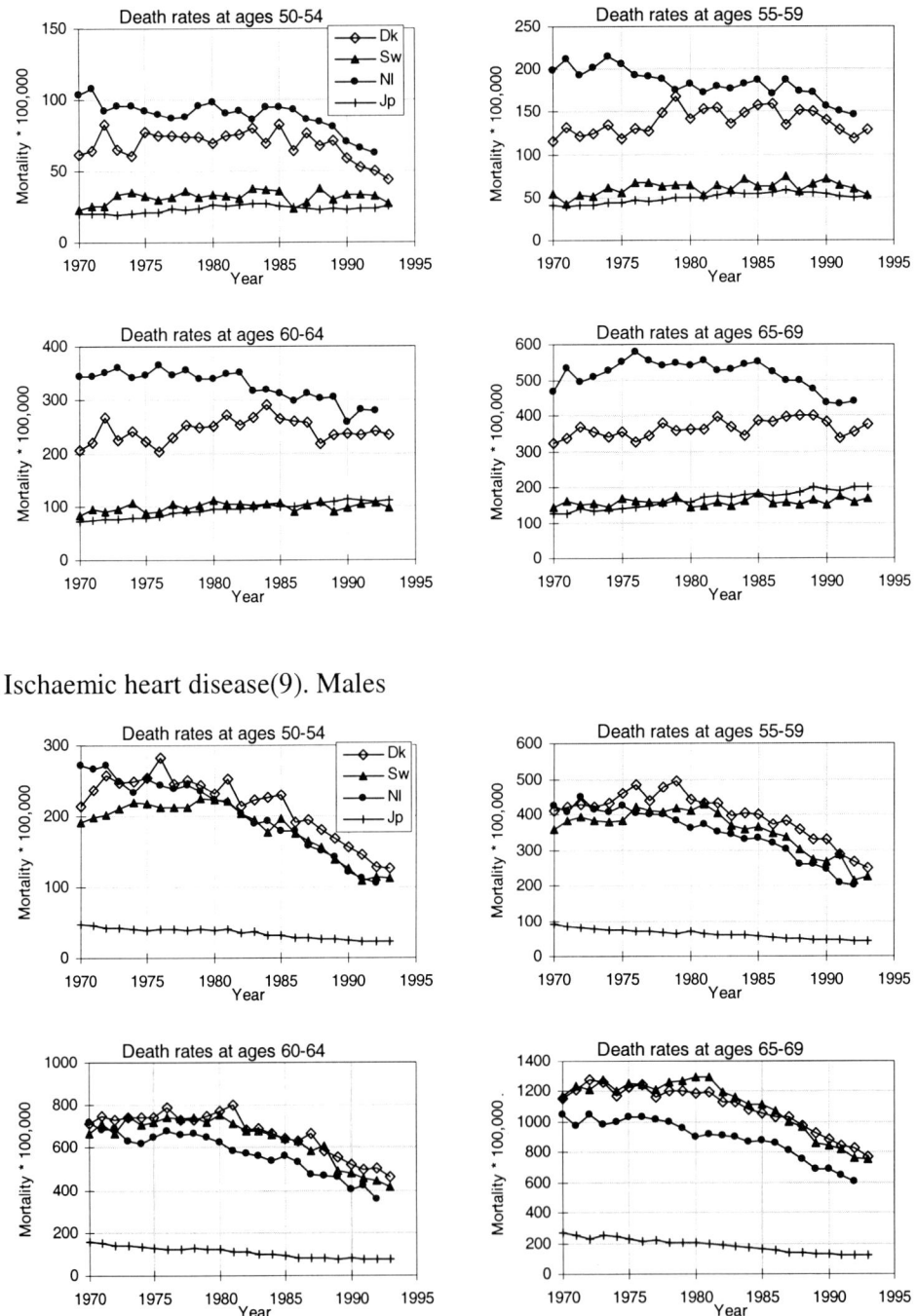

Figure 5.1(a) Disadvantageous trends in Danish cause-specific mortality. Males.

Bronchitis, emphysema and asthma(15). Males

Cirrhosis of liver(18). Males

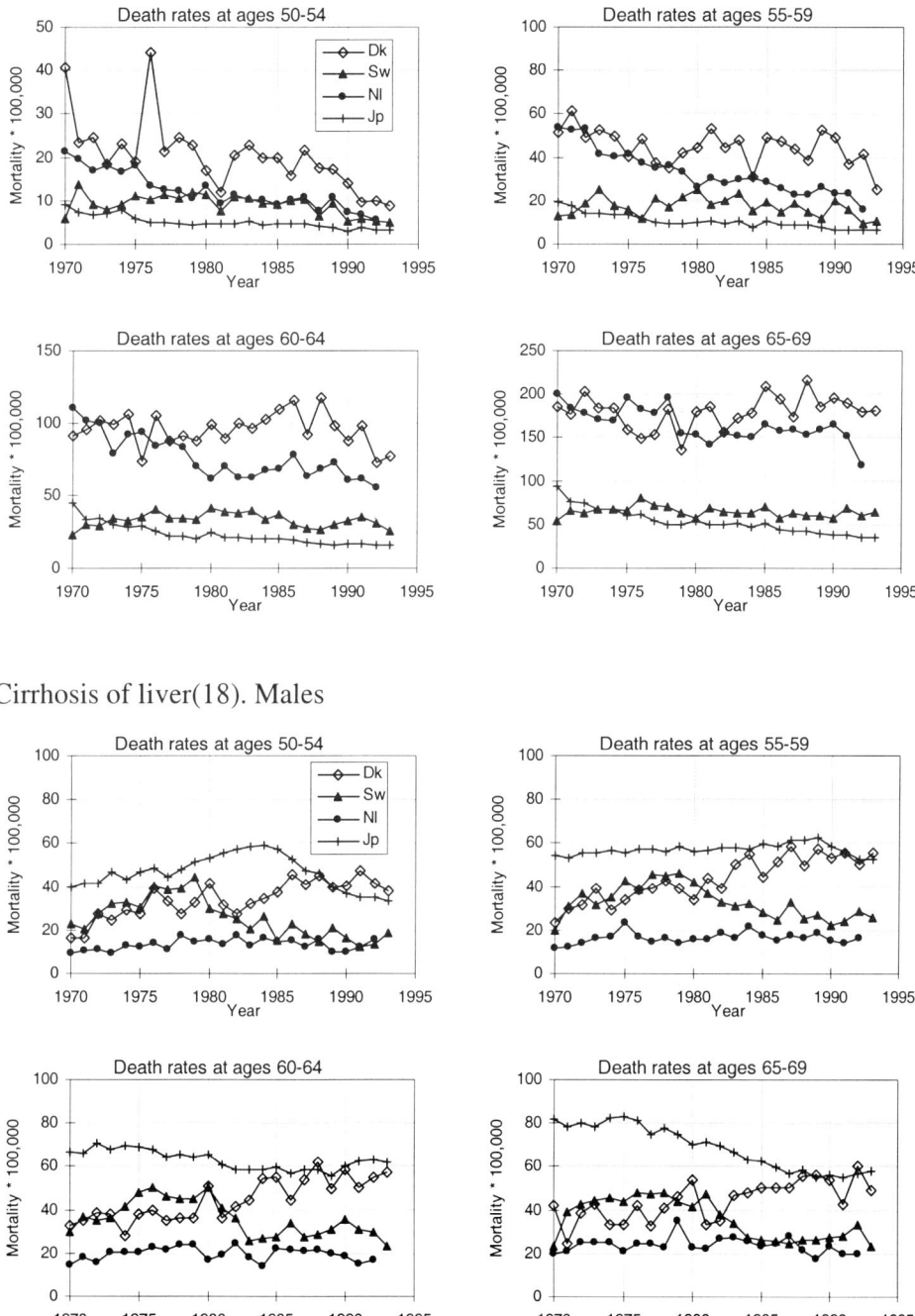

Figure 5.1(a) (cont.)

Suicide and self inflicted injury(21). Males

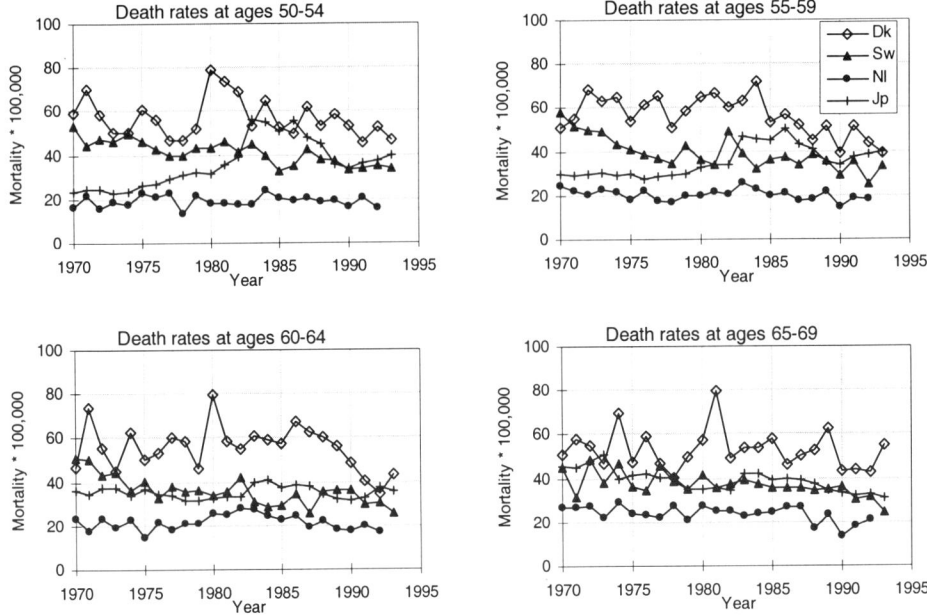

Figure 5.1(a) (cont.)

mortality levels in the Danish and Dutch populations, so there is much less difference between the two countries at the beginning of 1990s than in the 1970s. Moreover, there is a certain drop in the death rates at ages 50–54 for both Denmark and the Netherlands; this can perhaps be attributed to certain cohort effects, but this hypothesis requires additional elaboration.

Trends in death rates from ischaemic heart disease (9) followed almost the same trajectory in all European countries. Until 1980, the death rates remained at an approximately constant level, but after 1980, a persistent decline can be observed in all populations. The rate of decline was appreciable, and by the year 1993, the level of mortality had dropped to nearly half that of 1980. The level of mortality now differs considerably between countries and age groups. Even though it followed the same pattern of decline, in the lower age groups (50–54), Danish mortality was generally higher than that of Sweden and the Netherlands. In contrast, at higher ages (60–69), Danish and Swedish mortality curves are very close, while Dutch mortality is significantly lower. The exceptionally low level of Japanese mortality makes the position of this country outstanding in comparison. Mortality in Japan has also declined, but its level was significantly lower (4- to 6-fold) than in European countries.

Regarding respiratory diseases, we observe that there are no notable trends in Danish mortality from this cause of death. This is true of Sweden as well, although mortality in Denmark was on average 2.5 times higher than in Sweden. A comparison between Denmark and the Netherlands shows that in the early 1970s, mortality in both countries was nearly the same but in the early 1990s Danish death rates were about 50% higher because of the reductions in Dutch mortality. The death rates in Japan also show a downward trend, but their level was comparable with the Swedish level in the 1970s, which is appreciably lower than in the Netherlands. Because of this decline, the level of Japanese mortality in recent years has been the lowest of all countries included in the comparison.

In the case of cirrhosis of the liver (18), the trend in Danish mortality is the opposite of that observed in the other countries. I found a substantial and uniform increase in all age groups in Denmark, while mortality in Sweden dropped sharply in the early 1980s and mortality in Japan remained either constant (50–59) or declining (60–69). Even though Japanese mortality was remarkably higher than in the Nordic countries in 1970, the level of mortality in Denmark and in Japan was virtually the same in the 1993. Mortality in Sweden at that time was about half of that. In the Netherlands, no notable trends in mortality can be observed; it remained constant at low level.

Death rates from suicide (21) have traditionally been higher in Danish males than in other countries. There have been no considerable improvements here, except for some convergence to the levels of Sweden and the Netherlands at ages 55–64 in recent years. It is difficult to judge whether this is the onset of a general trend or some temporary phenomenon, because there is no evidence of a similar decline at ages 50–54 or 65–69.

In the populations of females, causes of deaths exhibiting unfavorable developments in Denmark, turn out to be the same as for males. Therefore, we will discuss the same causes of death as for males, adding only the trends in breast cancer. In the case of lung cancer mortality (2), there is a remarkable gap between the Danish population and other countries. Mortality from lung cancer has been increasing in all countries since 1970 and the rate of increase has been especially large in Europe (8.5% in Denmark and the Netherlands; 6.5% in Sweden) as opposed to Japan (1%). Mortality in Denmark, in the early 1970s, was appreciably higher than in other countries and this difference has increased in the 1990s, even though the Danish rate of increase was approximately the same as that of Sweden and the Netherlands.

Breast cancer death rates (7) have been gradually increasing in Denmark and

Malignant neoplasm of the trachea, bronchus and lungs(2). Females

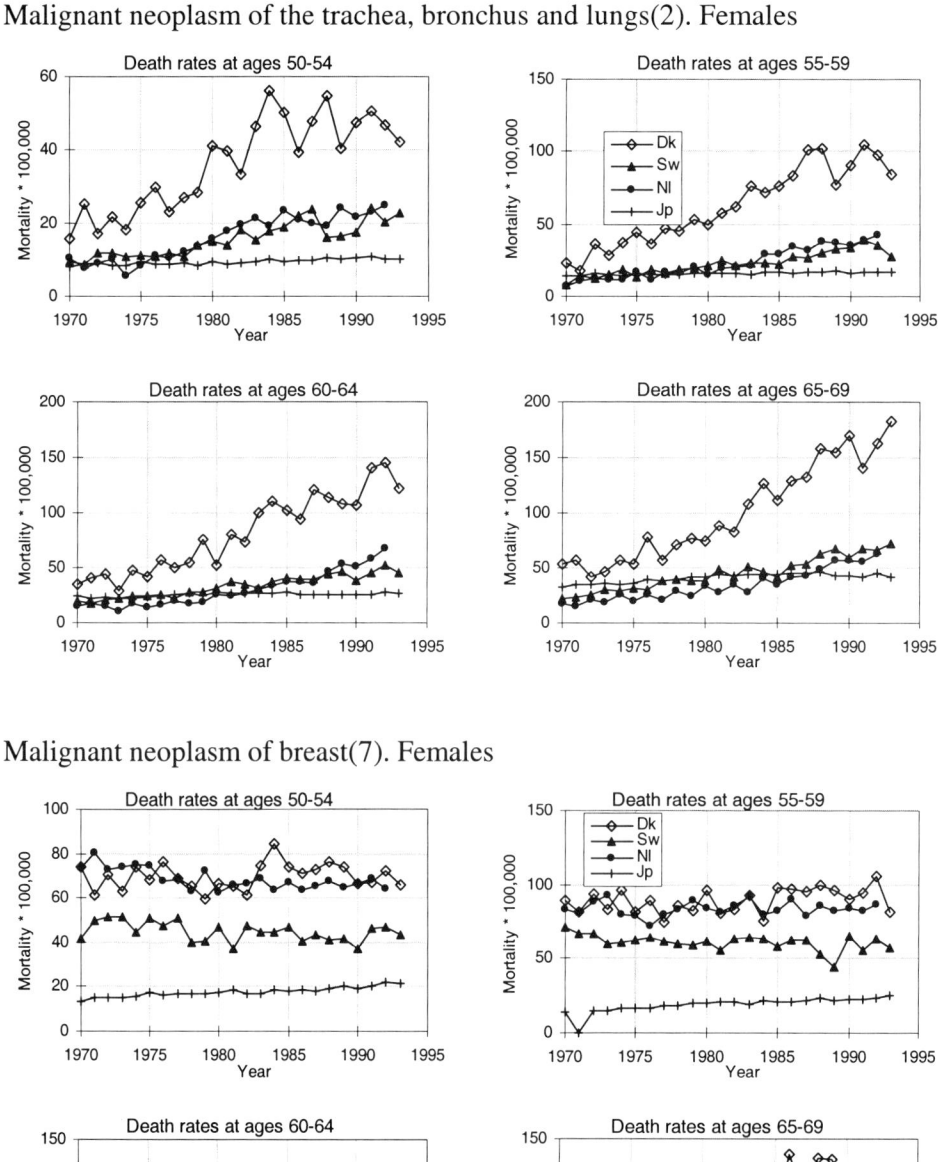

Malignant neoplasm of breast(7). Females

Figure 5.1(b) Disadvantageous trends in Danish cause-specific mortality. Females.

Ischaemic heart disease(9). Females

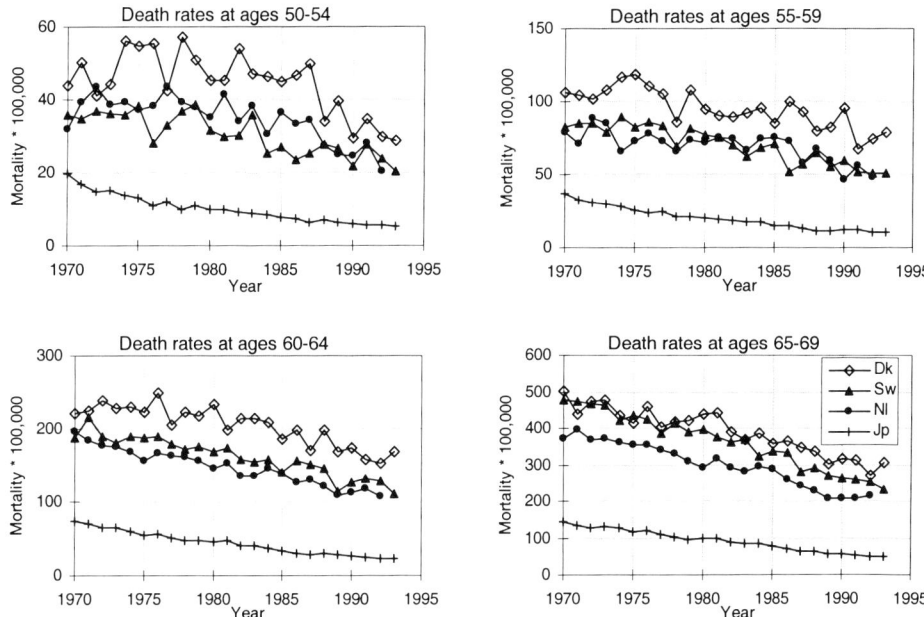

Bronchitis, emphysema and asthma(15). Females

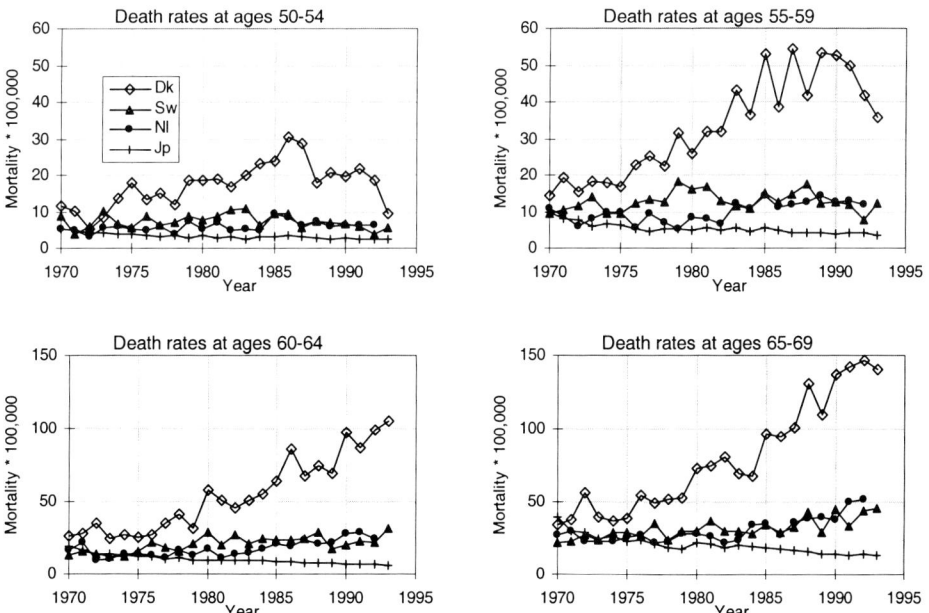

Figure 5.1(b) (cont.)

Cirrhosis of the liver(18). Females

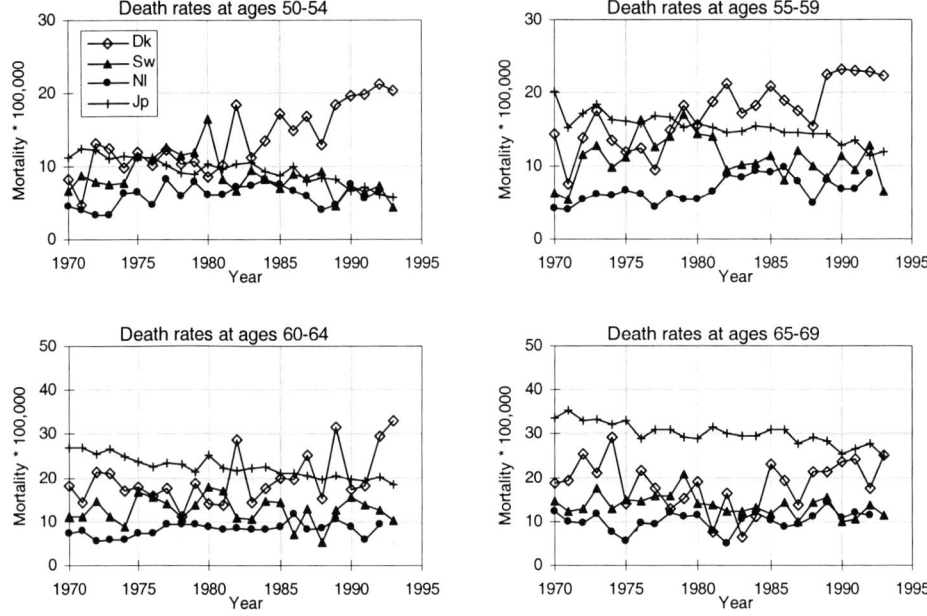

Suicide and self inflicted injury(21). Females

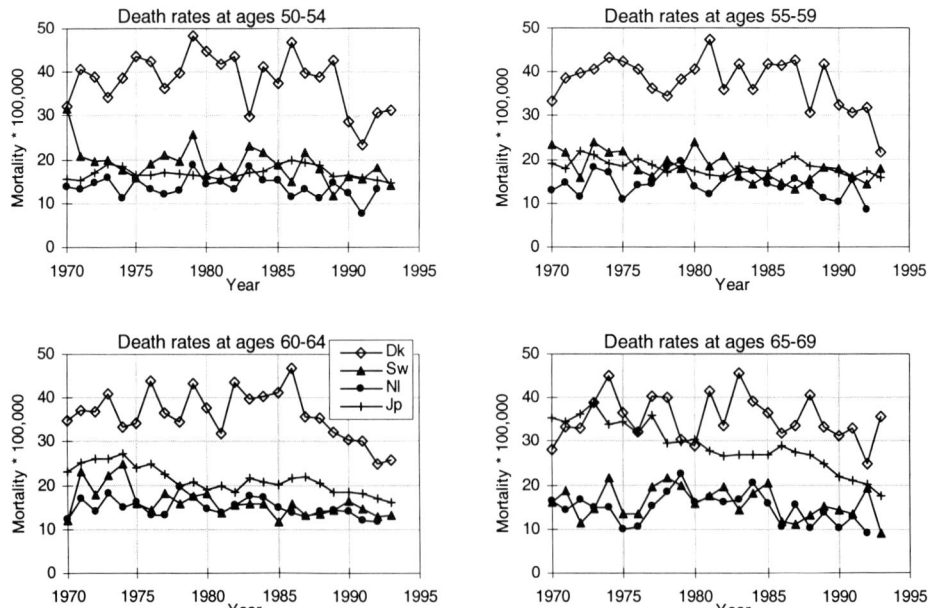

Figure 5.1(b) (cont.)

the Netherlands since 1970; this is especially noticeable in the higher age groups. The mortality differences from this cause of death are quite small in these countries, except during the last decade, where Danish mortality has been somewhat higher than Dutch mortality at ages 50–59. In contrast, Swedish death rates have been gradually declining since 1970, and so the gap between Swedish and Danish mortality has increased in recent years. Japanese mortality rates seem to be on the rise, but the level of Japanese mortality is much lower than in European countries.

Mortality developments as regards ischaemic heart disease (9) are close to the trends in the male populations, i.e., mortality has been declining in all populations, but the level of mortality in Denmark is higher. The main distinction seems to lie in the difference of mortality levels in Denmark as compared to other countries. This difference is far more eye-catching for females, than for males. This impression could be misleading, however, if we consider the contribution of (9) to the differences in life expectancy since the general level of mortality is significantly higher for males than for females.

Another group of diseases where Danish mortality was considerably higher than in the other countries includes bronchitis, emphysema and asthma (15). Mortality from this cause of death has increased dramatically in Denmark since 1970, when the level of Danish mortality was only slightly higher than in other countries. In contrast, mortality in other countries has either remained constant (60–69) or declined steadily (50–59). This development in mortality rates has led to a considerable excess of Danish mortality in recent years, which is especially remarkable in the age group 60–69. The pattern is very similar to the trends in lung cancer mortality, where a dramatic increase in Danish mortality can be observed. This finding suggests that there might be some correlation between lung cancer mortality and other diseases of the respiratory system. There may be some common factor contributing to this increase in mortality, such as smoking.

Mortality trends concerning cirrhosis of the liver (18) have been also unfavorable for Denmark, as was the case for males. While mortality in other countries has either declined or remained constant, the Danish rates have increased steadily. Particularly high mortality differences between Denmark and other countries in recent years are to be observed at ages 50–59. Since 1970, Danish death rates at these ages have approximately doubled. In the higher age groups both the increase and the differences between Denmark and other countries are less marked.

Suicide mortality (21) generally remained at a constant level in all countries from 1970 to 1993. There are only two exceptions. First, mortality at ages 65–69 in Japan declined significantly and reached the level of Sweden and the Netherlands in

1993. Second, there was a notable drop in Danish mortality at ages 60–64, starting in the year 1987. There was a similar decline in lower age groups (50–54 and 55–59), but this was less significant than in the age group 60–64. It is interesting to note that a similar drop in mortality can be observed on the male graph as well, which means that there might be some cohort effect operating in both the male and female populations. On the whole, the pattern of the excess Danish mortality is the same as for males, i.e., mortality levels have not changed very much, while Danish mortality is consistently higher than mortality in other countries. The mortality differences however are greater in the case of females.

The analysis conducted here permits us to draw some important conclusions. First of all, we must note that the structure of cause-specific mortality in excess Danish mortality is different for the male and female populations. Comparing male mortality rates with those of the Netherlands and Japan, we note that the most significant contribution to excess Danish mortality is added by cardiovascular diseases. Comparing Danish and Swedish rates, on the other hand, we see that cancer is the main factor involved in male mortality differences. In contrast, the results obtained from the analysis of the female populations suggest that the contributions from the different causes of death to the excess of Danish mortality are quite similar for all countries. It is evident from Table 5.2, that the most important contribution to excess female Danish mortality is that of cancer (especially lung and breast cancer).

An examination of trends in cause-specific mortality allowed us to discover those causes of death that contribute to excess Danish mortality. It turns out that these causes of death correspond closely for males and females (except for breast cancer), though their role in explaining the total mortality differences between Denmark and other countries is not the same. The most unfavorable trends involve diseases of the respiratory system: lung cancer, bronchitis, emphysema and asthma. Mortality from breast cancer also exhibits a negative trend, since it has increased in Denmark while it has declined in Sweden. Mortality from cirrhosis of the liver is also a concern, as rising trends have been observed in Denmark alone. This disease is usually linked to the consumption of alcohol, which is for example, significantly higher in Denmark than in Sweden. Finally, I would like to mention the importance of mortality differences as regards ischaemic heart disease. Although the trends in Danish mortality have been in concordance with the developments in other countries, I found that the Danes have somehow lagged behind their European counterparts, since the Danish death rate remains consistently on a higher level. Since mortality from this cause of death is considerably higher than from other diseases, it might provide a main contribution, if the differences in life expectancy are analyzed.

6. Conclusions and further research

6.1 Main results

It is well known that the life expectancy in Denmark has increased significantly since the middle of 19th century. The age-specific mortality changes are less well-known, since investigation thereof has been hampered by a lack of data and convenient visualization tools. Such data are now available and can be obtained from the Danish mortality database. They are also included in the Human Mortality Database[19], which is a joint project between Max Planck Institute for Demographic Research, Germany and University of California, Berkeley, USA, and will be available through the Internet in the year 2002. The visualization program to produce demographic contour maps has also been developed by K. Andreev and distributed free of charge with his PhD thesis (Andreev, 1999). All contour maps presented in this monograph were produced with the help of this program.

The first objective of this work was the compilation of a consistent Danish mortality database, which includes data on population and deaths for the period 1835–2000 and for all ages. As similar databases are likely to be constructed in the future for other countries and regions, the process of compilation was described in detail. Special attention was given to the methods of reconstructing missing population data and redistributing the death counts. Some of the methods described in Chapter 2, will be included in methodology of Human Mortality Database and the accompanying software library, which are currently under development. This will facilitate the application of methods for estimating mortality surfaces in other populations.

The second objective was to demonstrate the potential importance of the Danish mortality data for demographic research. I focused on the investigation of the Danish mortality surface and Danish population surface, with special attention given to the age-specific changes. Lexis maps related to population changes, helped us to explore the population developments on age-specific basis. Primary attention was paid to the dynamics of population aging in the recent decades. Striking increases are to be observed in the population of the elderly, which is now the fastest growing segment in the Danish population. The research also stresses the importance of cohort effects in the population dynamics. One of the outstanding examples of cohort effects is the generation of baby boomers, who are now about 55 years old. These cohorts partially relieved the population pressure of the elderly (Fig. 3.4), but this

---

[19] Temporary name.

beneficial situation is temporary and will last only for about another 10 years, until they too become pensioners.

As regards mortality evolution, contour maps of Danish mortality (Fig. 3.8) and maps of rates of mortality changes over time (Fig. 3.9) allowed us to identify the timing and the age-specific structure of the mortality transition. The results of the analysis suggest that mortality transition in Denmark at the end of the 19th century belonged to the mainstream of transitions in other European countries. In fact, the Danish mortality changes were more favorable than in other countries. Consequently, Danish life expectancy was among the highest in Europe at the beginning of 20th century. Nonetheless, a comprehensive study of factors behind the Danish mortality transition and the role they played in the observed mortality decline has yet to be carried out.

Until the 1960s, mortality in Denmark declined very rapidly, and life expectancy rose to exceptionally high levels, which were unprecedented in Danish history. Then progress in the mortality decline decelerated significantly and the pace of increase in life expectancy fell down to remarkably low levels. Despite stagnation or even a degree increase in mortality in middle ages, life expectancy continued to grow at a low pace, because of the rapid mortality reductions at oldest-old ages and continuing mortality decline in infancy and childhood ages. Such mortality development was unusual when compared with mortality trends observed in other European countries, where gains in life expectancy were appreciably higher since the 1960s (Chapter 4).

Faced with these developments, the Danish government set up a committee to investigate the slowdown in the increase of expectation of life. The project has been carried out by Danish Ministry of Health in 1993 and as a result fourteen books were published in 1993 and 1994 (Sundhedsministeriets Middellevetidsudvalg, 1993). The investigation focused mainly on trends in the standardized mortality rates, social-economic variables and the analysis of differences in life styles. Despite the large volume of the material presented, the age-specific mortality differences did not receive the proper amount of attention in this study. Nonetheless, this analysis can shed some light on which age groups have experienced more excess mortality and on the time when the problems started to emerge.

In order to investigate age-specific mortality differences, I estimated the surfaces of ratios of Danish mortality to those of other nine countries (Chapter 4). This permitted me to identify the area with excess Danish mortality and to follow the age- and time-specific dynamics of the mortality ratios. The results of this analysis suggest that the area of excess mortality for females began to form in the late 1960s, at the age of 50–60. Over time, the area with plus mortality spread out to lower and higher age groups, thus making for more striking mortality differences. This pattern of development in the death rate ratios prevailed until the latest years for which data were available, and so far there are no favorable tendencies to be observed. For males, the developments were similar, except for the fact that the excess of Danish mortality was less pronounced and occurred later in time.

Finally, I analyzed cause-specific mortality in order to explore the relative contribution of the different causes of death to the excess of Danish mortality. I decomposed the total excess mortality for the years starting with 1985 and for the age groups where the highest mortality differences has been observed (50–69). This analysis provided useful insight into the cause-specific structure of the excess Danish mortality. It was found that for females, the main contribution to the excess of Danish mortality was provided by cancer, especially by lung and breast cancers. The pattern was remarkably stable among all populations involved in the comparison. For males, however, it varied between causes of death. Cardiovascular diseases were the most important cause of excess Danish mortality compared with the male populations of the Netherlands and Japan, while in case of Sweden the most significant differences were observed in cancer mortality.

6.2 Further research

Further research should be based on the biostatistical analysis of survival data on risk factors, i.e., smoking, alcohol consumption, etc. It would also be helpful to incorporate social-economic and life-style variables, e.g. GDP, unemployment rates, fat consumption etc.: the variables known to be correlated with death rates. Such an analysis is not straightforward enough to carry out and main two reasons are as follows.

The first is that a) our knowledge about the relationship between mortality and risk factors is not precise and b) a reliable analytical model has not yet been developed, that would specify the influence of the risk factors on mortality, taking into account the interdependencies between variables and the lagged time effects.

The second reason, is the lack of adequate data; the data on social-economic variables are usually only available in relation to the total population. In other words, the age distribution is unknown. As shown above, excess Danish mortality has not been uniform over age, and the highest mortality differences are to be observed at ages 50–70. It could be the case that the effect of a social-economic variable depends on age. It could be harmful in one age group and beneficial in another. In this case, the age structure of this variable must be known in order to account correctly for the effect of this factor.

In addition, time series should start well back before 1970, when the excess Danish mortality first became evident. The effect of a risk factor on mortality could be lagged rather than instantaneous, so the reason for the currently observed excess mortality can lie far back in the past. This follows from a pilot study, which was accomplished in order to survey the trends in alcohol and tobacco consumption. The data were extracted from the OECD Health database[20] and the trends are shown in Fig. 6.1 and Fig. 6.2.

As indicated by Fig. 6.1, there was a sharp increase in the annual consumption of alcohol in Denmark in the period from 1960 to 1975; the number of liters per capita rose from 5.5 in 1960 to 12 in 1975. Consumption has remained at this high level ever since. Alcohol consumption in Sweden, on the other hand, rose from about 5 liters in 1960 to 7.5 liters in 1975, only to drop to the level of 6 liters per capita sometime later. The timing of observed differences in the annual consumption of alcohol corresponds well to the timing of the emergence of excess Danish mortality.

It might be the case that the high levels of alcohol consumption have an immediate effect on health and mortality of general population. This hypothesis can be tested with the data from other countries, in which governmental interventions or anti-alcohol campaigns have taken place to reduce the level of alcohol consumption. In Russia, for example, the sale of alcohol was restricted in 1985–1986 and alcohol production was significantly reduced. This resulted in an immediate increase in life expectancy. If in the years 1983–1984, life expectancy at birth was 62.00 years for males and 73.31 for females, during the years of the anti-alcohol campaign it rose to 64.91 for males and 74.55 for females (1986–1987). With the end of the anti-alcohol campaign, the level of consumption increased again and life expectancy fell to 63.79 for males and 74.27 for females (year 1990) (Goskomstat of Russia, 1996). The gain in the male life expectancy during the anti-alcohol campaign is striking.

Consumption of tobacco in Denmark has been declining since 1970. In contrast, it increased in Japan, so that in 1983, the consumption was at the same level in the two countries. Since then tobacco consumption has been higher in Japan than in Denmark (in 1995 the levels of consumption were 3200 and 2300 grams per capita, respectively). Nonetheless, the gap between Danish and Japanese mortality has continued to grow since 1983. This suggests that the level of tobacco consumption has a lagged effect on survival and can be observed only at some point later in time.

Tobacco consumption in Denmark received a great amount of attention in a recent report from the Danish Ministry of Health (Sundhedsministeriets Middel-

---

[20] http://www.oecd.org/els/health/

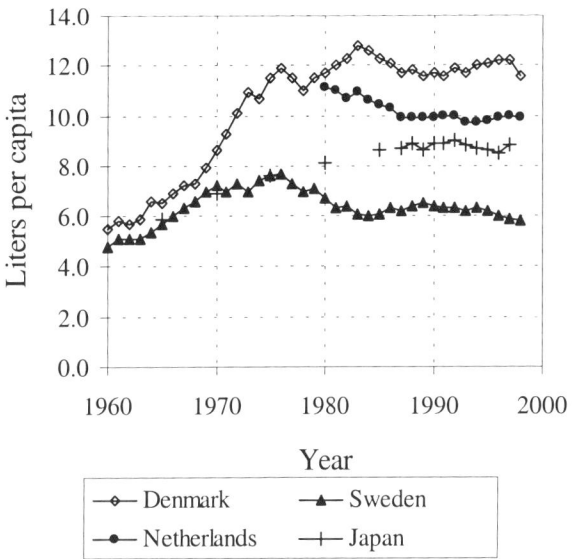

Figure 6.1. Annual consumption of alcohol (population aged 15 and over)

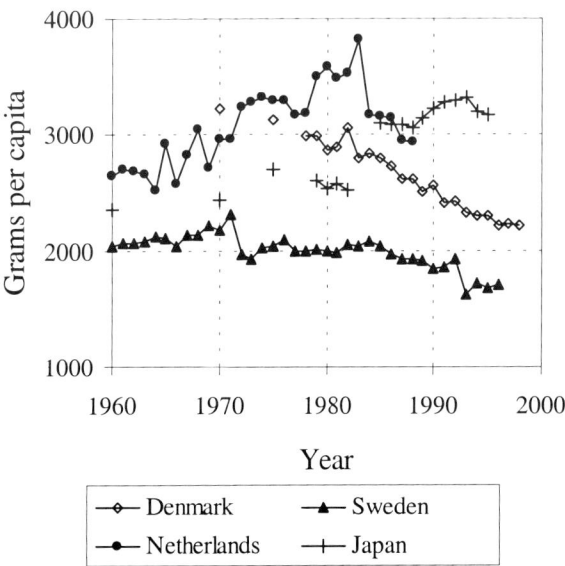

Figure 6.2. Annual consumption of tobacco (population aged 15 and over)

levetidsudvalg, 1998). According to this report, tobacco-related mortality is responsible for a considerable part of the negative development in Danish life expectancy. If tobacco-related mortality were eliminated, life expectancy would rise by three years in Denmark. Findings in Chapter 5 support this hypothesis, as diseases of the respiratory system are the most important contributors to excess Danish mortality. However, the relative importance of this factor is perhaps exaggerated in this report as when compared with other factors, i.e. the consumption of alcohol.

Further research will significantly benefit from a deeper investigation of the mortality differences between Denmark and Sweden. It seems to be preferable to focus only on two countries, rather than try to include many of them. There are well-known similarities between these countries, so we can exclude a large number of factors that otherwise might be hypothesized to account for mortality differences. An investigation of differences in the health care systems and in preventive intervention should also prove valuable for determining factors behind the higher mortality in Denmark. It seems that even minor differences can have a profound effect on mortality. Such a study should prove to be important not only for the Danish society; but it would also provide a significant contribution to mortality research.

References

Aarssen, K. and de Haan, L. On the Maximal Life Span of Humans. Mathematical Population Studies. 1994; 4(4):259-281.

Andersen, Otto. Dødelighedsforholdene i Danmark 1735-1839. Særtryk Af Nationaløkonomisk Tidsskrift; 1973; Statistisk Institut, Københavns Universitet.

Andreev, K. F. Sex differentials in survival in the Canadian population, 1921-1997: A descriptive analysis with focus on age-specific structure. Demographic Research. 2000 Dec 13; 3(12).

Andreev, K. F. Demographic surfaces: Estimation, Assessment and Presentation, with Application to Danish Mortality, 1835–1995. Ph.D. thesis: University of Southern Denmark; 1999.

Bjerregaard, P. and Juel, K. Middellevetid og dødlighed i Danmark. UGESKR Læger. 1993 Dec 13; 155(50).

Bjerregaard, P. and Juel, K. Middellevetid og dødelighed. En analyse af dødeligheden i Danmark og nogle europæiske lande, 1950-1990. København, Dansk Institut for Klinisk Epidemiologi: Middellevetidsudvalget; 1994.

Caselli, G.; Vallin, J., Vaupel, J., and Yashin, A. Age-Specific Mortality Trends in France and Italy Since 1900: Period and Cohort Effects. European Journal of Population. 1987; 3:33-60.

Caselli, G., Vaupel, J., and Yashin, A. Mortality in Italy: Contours of a Century of Evoution. Paper Presented at Session F.8 of IUSSP International Population Conference, Florence 7-12 June, 1985. 1985.

Chiang, Chin Long. The Life Table and its applications. Robert E. Krieger Publishing Company, Inc; 1984; ISBN: 0-89874-570-5.

Christensen, Kaare; Vaupel, James W.; Holm, Niels V., and Yashin, Anatoli I. Mortality among twins after age 6: fetal origins hypothesis versus twin method. British Medical Journal. 1995 Feb; 310(6977):432-435. ISSN: 0959-8138.

Condran, Gretchen A., Himes, Christine L., and Preston, Samuel H. Old-Age Mortality Patterns in Low-Mortality Countries: an Evaluation of Population and Death Data at Advanced, 1950 to the Present. Population Bulletin of the United Nations. 1991; 30:23-59.

Curtsinger, J., Fukui, H., Townsend, D., and Vaupel, J. Demography of genotypes: Failures of the limited life-span paradigm in Drosophila melanogaster. Science. 1992; 28:461-463.

Dierckx, Paul. Curve and Surface Fitting with Splines. United States: Oxford university Press Inc., New York; 1993; ISBN: 0-19-853441-8.

Fries, J. Aging, Natural Death, and Compression of Morbidity. The New England Journal of Medicine. 1980 Jul 17; 303(3):130-135.

Goskomstat of Russia. The Demographic Yearbook of Russia. 1996.

Hvidt, Kristian. Flugten til Amerika eller Drivkrafter i masseudvandringen fra Danmark 1868-1914.; 1971.

Impagliazzo, John. Deterministic Aspects of Mathematical Demography.: November 1984;

Johansen, H. C. and Boje, P. Working Class Housing in Odense 1750-1914. Scandinavian Economic History Review. 1986; 34(2):132-52.

Johansen, H. C. The Development of Reporting Systems for Causes of Deaths in Denmark. Unpublished Paper. 1996.

Johansen, H. C. Early Danish Parish Registers. Danish Center for Demographic Research. Research Report 3. 1998. ISSN: 1398-4292.

Juel, Knud and Sjol, Anette. Decline in Mortality from Heart Disease in Denmark : some Methodological Problems. Journal of Clinical Epidemiology. 1995; 48(4):467-472.

Kannisto, V., Lauritsen, J., Thatcher, R., and Vaupel, J. Reductions in Mortality at Advanced Ages: Several Decades of Evidence from 27 Countries. Population and Development Review. 1994 Dec; 20(4):793-810. ISSN: 0098-7921.

Lancaster, H. O. Expectations of Life : A Study in the Demography, Statistics, and History of World Mortality. New York: Springer; 1990.

Legge, Thomas M. Public Health in European Capitals. London; 1896.

Madsen, Th. and Madsen, S. Diphtheria in Denmark. From 23,695 to 1 case - Post or propter. I. Serum therapy. II. Diphtheria immunization. Dan. Med. Bul. 1956; 3:112-21.

Borgan, Jens-Kristian. Kohort-dodeligheten i Norge 1846-1980. Central Bureau of Statistics of Norway; 1983 Nov 15.

Matthiessen, Poul C. Some aspects of the demographic transition in Denmark. Copenhagen: Copenhagen University; 1970; ISBN: 87 505 0091 0.

McKeown, T. The Modern Rise of Population. London; 1976.

McNeil, Donald R.; Trussel, James T.; Turner, John C. Spline Interpolation of Demographic Data. Readings in Population Research Methodology. Volume 1. Basic Tools. Reprinted from Demography 14, 2 (1977). pp. 245-52. 1993.

Preston, Samuel H.; Elo, Irma T., and Stewart, Quincy. Effects of age misreporting on mortality estimates at older ages. Population Studies. 1999; (53):165-177.

Schofield, R. Ed., Reher, D. S. Ed., and Bideau, A. Ed. The Decline of Mortality in Europe. Oxford: Clarendon Press; 1991.

Shryock, Henry S., Siegel, Jacob. Selected General Methods. Readings in Population Research Methodology. Volume 1. Basic Tools.; 1993.

Smith, E. The Peasant's Home 1760-1875. London; 1876.

Sundhedsministeriet. Danskernes dødelighed i 1990'erne. 1. delrapport fra Middellevetidsudvalget. Nyt Nordisk Forlag Arnold Busck A/S; 1998 Dec; ISBN: 87-17-06878-9. http://www.sum.dk/publika/dodeligh/index.htm

Sundhedsministeriets Middellevetidsudvalg. Danmark. Rapport. Komplet 1-14. København: Middellevetidsudvalget; 1993; ISBN: 87-601-4108-5.

Tabeau, Ewa, Frans van Poppel, and Willekens, Frans. Mortality in the Netherlands: The Data Base. The Hague; 1994; ISBN: 90-70990-46-6.

Vallin, Jacques. La Mortalité par Génération en France. depuis 1899. Paris: Presses Universitaires de France; 1973. 483 pp (Travaux et Documents).

Vandeschrick, Christophe. The Lexis diagram, a misnomer. 2001 Sep 3; 4; http://www.demographic-research.org/.

Vaupel, J. W., Zhenglian, W., Andreev, K. F., and Yashin, A. I. Population Data at Glance: Shaded Contour Maps of Demographic Surfaces over Age and Time. Odense University, Denmark: Odense University Press; 1998; ISBN: 87-7838-338-2; http://www.demogr.mpg.de/Papers/Books/Monograph4/PopData1.htm.

Vincent, Paul. La Mortalité des vieillards. Population. 1951; 6(2):181-204.

Yashin, A. I., Vaupel, J. W., Andreev, K. F., Tan, Q., Iachine, I. A., Carotenuto, L.; De Benedictis, G.; Bonafe, M., Valensin, S., and Franceschi, C. Combining genetic and demographic information in population studies of aging and longevity. Journal of Epidemiology and Biostatistics. 1998; 3(3):289-294.

Appendix

Appendix Table 1. Earlier publications of Danish population statistics.

Appendix Table 2. Raw population data used for construction of the Danish mortality database.

Appendix Table 3. Raw death counts data used for construction of the Danish mortality database.

Appendix Table 4. The average deviation between the genuine and interpolated death distributions for the years 1916, 1921–1940.

Appendix 5. Kernel smoothing of Lexis maps.

Appendix 6. Estimating surface of the rate of mortality changes over time.

Appendix 7. Estimating surface of ratio of death rates over age and time.

Appendix Table 8. List of causes of deaths selected for the analysis of mortality differences.

Appendix 9. Contents of the accompanying CD-ROM.

Appendix Table 1. Earlier publications of Danish population statistics (reproduced from Befolkningens Bevægelser 1999, Danmarks Statistik).

Statistisk tabelværk (Table Works)		Vielser, fødsler og dødsfald (Marriages, Births and Deaths)			
1801–33:	I,1	1870–74:	IV A,1	1906–10:	IV A,8
1834–39:	I,6	1875–79:	IV A,2	1911–15:	IV A,13
1840–44:	I,10	1880–84:	IV A,5	1916–20:	IV A,15
1845–49:	II,1	1885–89:	IV A,7	1921–25:	IV A,17
1850–54:	II,17,1.del	1890–94:	IV A,9	1926–30:	IV A,19
1855–59:	III,2	1895–1900:	V A,2	1931–40:	IV A,22
1860–64:	III,12	19.årh.:*	V A,5	1941–55:	1962:I
1865–69:	III,25	1901–05:	V A,6	1956–69:	1973:XI

*Befolkningsforholdene i Danmark i det 19.århundrede.

Statistiske meddelelser		Befolkningens bevægelser (Population movements)			
1931–33:	4,95,4	1946: 4,126,6	1958: 1960:2	1970: 1972:7
1934:	4,97,6	1947: 4,133,3	1959: 1961:1	1971: 1973:10
1935:	4,100,4	1948: 4,138,3	1960: 1962:8	1972: 1974:9
1936:	4,102,5	1949: 4,143,4	1961: 1963:5	1973: 1975:9
1937:	4,106,5	1950: 4,147,2	1962: 1964:5	1974: 1976:5
1938:	4,109,3	1951: 4,150,3	1963: 1965:5	1975: 1977:4
1939:	4,110,5	1952: 4,154,2	1964: 1966:4	1976: 1978:1
1940:	4,111,5	1953: 4,157,4	1965: 1967:7	1977: 1978:12
1941:	4,155,5	1954: 4,161,4	1966: 1968:6	1978: 1980:3
1942:	4,119,4	1955: 4,166,3	1967: 1969:1	1979: 1981:1
1943:	4,120,5	1956: 4,167,2	1968: 1970:4	1980: 1982:1
1944–45:	4,125,4	1957: 4,173,2	1969: 1971:3	

Årspublikationer (Annual publications) — Befolkningens bevægelser (Population movements)

1981 pub.1983	1986 pub.1988	1991 pub.1993	1996 pub.1998
1982 pub.1984	1987 pub.1989	1992 pub.1994	1997 pub.1999
1983 pub.1985	1988 pub.1990	1993 pub.1995	1998 pub.2000
1984 pub.1986	1989 pub.1991	1994 pub.1996	
1985 pub.1987	1990 pub.1992	1995 pub.1997	

Appendix Table 2.
Raw population data used for construction of the Danish mortality database.

Period	Age groups	Reference
1801	0–10, 10–20 ... 100+	Befolkningsforholdene i Danmark i det 19. aarhundrede. Census.
1834		
1840	0–1, 1–3, 3–5, 5–10, ... 110+	Census.
1845		
1850	0–1, 1–3, 3–5, 5–7, 7–10, 10–15, ... 100+	Census.
1855	0–1, 1–3, 3–5, 5–6, 6–7, 7–10, 10–14, 14–15 ... 24–25, 25–30 ... 100+	Census.
1860		
1870	0–1, 1–2 ... 100+	Befolkningsforholdene i Danmark i det 19. aarhundrede. Census.
1880		
1890		
1901		
1906–1940	0–1 ... 85+	Estimates from Danmarks Statistik.
1941–1970	0–1 ... 100+	Estimates from Danmarks Statistik.
1971–1975	0–90+	Befolkningens bevægelser. Danmarks Statistik. KBH.
	90–99+	Befolkningen i kommunerne pr 1. Januar.
1976–1991	0–1 ...	Befolkningens bevægelser. Danmarks Statistik.
1992–1993	0–1 ...	Befolkningens bevægelser. Danmarks Statistik.
1994	0–100	Danmarks Statistik. Befolknings bevægelser 1993.
	100+	Provided by A. Skytthe, University of Southern Denmark. Originally from Danish CPR register.
1995	0–100	Danmarks Statistik. Befolknings bevægelser 1994.
	100+	Provided by V. Kannisto.
1996	0–100	Danmarks Statistik. Befolknings bevægelser 1995.
	100+	Provided by V. Kannisto.
1997	all ages	Danmarks Statistik. Befolknings bevægelser 1997.
1998	all ages	Danmarks Statistik. Befolknings bevægelser 1998.
1999	all ages	Danmarks Statistik. Befolknings bevægelser 1999.
2000	all ages	Danmarks Statistik. Befolknings bevægelser 1999.

Appendix Table 3.

Raw death counts data used for construction of the Danish mortality database.

Period	Age	Source
1835–1854	0–1, 1–3, 3–5, 5–10 ... 110+	Statistik Tabelværk, various publications.
1855–1869	0–1, ... 4–5, 5–10 ... 100+	Statistik Tabelværk, various publications. Detailed statistics for the first year of age are available.
1870–1915	0–1 ... 4–5, 5–10 ... 95–100, 100+	Statistik Tabelværk.
1916–1920	0,1,2 .. 100+	Statistik Tabelværk.
1921–1942	0,1,2 .. 100+ by year and cohort.	Statistik Tabelværk. Befolkningens bevægelser.
1943–1999	All ages by year and cohort.	Befolkningens bevægelser. If death counts were not published for ages 100 and above, they have been obtained directly from Danmarks Statistik.

Appendix Table 4.

The average deviation between the genuine and interpolated death distributions for the years 1916, 1921–1940.

Deviation equation	Interpolation scheme					
	Sprague	Beers Ordinary	Beers Modified	Karup-King	Cubic spline	5th order spline
	Males					
(A.1)	6.403e-03	6.283e-03	5.998e-03	6.100e-03	**5.627e-03**	5.765e-03
(A.2)	6.431e-03	6.247e-03	6.196e-03	6.238e-03	**5.751e-03**	5.870e-03
(A.3)	1.097e-06	1.089e-06	1.137e-06	1.139e-06	**1.087e-06**	1.101e-06
(A.4)	1.092e-06	1.085e-06	1.137e-06	1.133e-06	**1.084e-06**	1.099e-06
(A.5)	6.368e-05	6.274e-05	6.466e-05	6.491e-05	**6.144e-05**	6.239e-05
	Females					
(A.1)	5.736e-03	5.455e-03	5.319e-03	5.398e-03	**5.042e-03**	5.226e-03
(A.2)	5.774e-03	5.466e-03	5.552e-03	5.636e-03	**5.190e-03**	5.343e-03
(A.3)	1.004e-06	**9.944e-07**	1.053e-06	1.071e-06	1.000e-06	1.026e-06
(A.4)	1.011e-06	**1.002e-06**	1.066e-06	1.080e-06	1.008e-06	1.034e-06
(A.5)	5.624e-05	5.529e-05	5.771e-05	5.839e-05	**5.483e-05**	5.623e-05

The bold-faced values in each row of this table show the minimal deviation (best results) among all interpolation schemes.

Equations used to compute the deviation δ between the original and interpolated death distributions:

$$\delta = \frac{1}{n} \sum_{y=y_{min}}^{y_{max}} \sum_{x=5}^{99} \frac{(p_o(x,y) - p_i(x,y))^2}{p_i(x,y)}$$

(A.1)

$$\delta = \frac{1}{n} \sum_{y=y_{min}}^{y_{max}} \sum_{x=5}^{99} \frac{(p_o(x,y) - p_i(x,y))^2}{p_o(x,y)}$$

(A.2)

$$\delta = \frac{1}{n} \sum_{y=y_{min}}^{y_{max}} \sum_{x=5}^{99} (p_o(x,y) - p_i(x,y))^2 \, p_i(x,y)$$

(A.3)

$$\delta = \frac{1}{n} \sum_{y=y_{min}}^{y_{max}} \sum_{x=5}^{99} (p_o(x,y) - p_i(x,y))^2 \, p_o(x,y)$$

(A.4)

$$\delta = \frac{1}{n} \sum_{y=y_{min}}^{y_{max}} \sum_{x=5}^{99} (p_o(x,y) - p_i(x,y))^2$$

(A.5)

where $p_o(x,y), p_i(x,y)$ are proportions of the original and the interpolated death distributions at age x and year y, and n is the total number of years used in summing up.

Appendix 5. Kernel smoothing of Lexis maps.

Let $m_{i,j}$ be an element of the matrix used to produce a Lexis map in which i is the row index and j is the column index. Usually i denotes the current age and j is the current year but this is not required. The $m_{i,j}$ itself can be any demographic indicator such as central death rate, population level, mortality ratio etc. In this method the value of $m_{i,j}$ is replaced by the weighted average of the $(2k+1)^2$ values in the $2k+1$ square of points:

(A.6)
$$m^*_{i,j} = \sum_{x=i-k}^{x=i+k} \sum_{y=j-k}^{y=j+k} w_{x,y} m_{x,y}$$

The weights $w_{i,j}$ can be computed by selecting a bivariate kernel function $K(x,y)$. Using this kernel function we can select any size k of the smoothing matrix and compute the weighting matrix $w_{i,j}$:

$$w_{i,j} = \int_{i^*}^{i^*+h} \int_{j^*}^{j^*+h} K(x,y) dx dy$$

(A.7)

where $h = \dfrac{2}{2k+1}$, $i^* = (i-1)h - 1$, $j^* = (j-1)h - 1$ and $i, j \in [1,2,..2k+1]$.

A convenient choice would be the bivariate Epanechnikov kernel $K(x,y) = 0.75^2(1-x^2)(1-y^2)$. In this case the 3x3 smoothing matrix is as follows

$$w_{i,j} = \begin{matrix} 0.06722 & 0.12483 & 0.06722 \\ 0.12483 & 0.23182 & 0.12483 \\ 0.06722 & 0.12483 & 0.06722 \end{matrix}.$$

Appendix 6. Estimating surface of the rate of mortality changes over time.

Let

$$m_{x,y} = \frac{D_{x,y}}{P_{x,y}}$$

(A.8)

be the central death rate at age x and year y, where $D_{x,y}$ is the death counts in the Lexis rectangle and $P_{x,y}$ is the population estimate in the middle of the year y. In order to estimate mortality progress I select death rates in k preceding years and k following years and at the same age x. I also assume that mortality changes exponentially during the period $[y-k, y+k]$:

$$\ln m_{x,y} = \ln m_x + \rho_{x,y} Y$$

(A.9)

where Y is the current year, $\rho_{x,y}$ is rate of mortality change over time at age x and year y (this parameter will be negative if mortality is declining and positive if it is increasing) and m_x is the death rate at $Y = 0$ (for estimation purposes it is recommended that the variable Y be normalized by subtracting the current year y).

Parameter estimates are obtained by maximizing the Poisson loglikelihood function:

$$L = \sum_{Y=y-k}^{Y=y+k} D_Y (\ln m_x + \rho_{x,y} Y) - P_Y e^{\ln m_x + \rho_{x,y} Y}$$

(A.10)

Hypothesis $\rho_{x,y} = 0$ can be tested with the likelihood ratio test.

Appendix 7. Estimating surface of ratio of death rates over age and time.

Let $m_{x,y}$ and $m^*_{x,y}$ be the central death rates in the first population and in the second population, respectively. Let $w_{i,j}$ be the weighting matrix generated by some kernel $K(x, y)$ (Appendix 5). We can employ Poisson regression to estimate the ratio $r_{x,y}$ of two mortality surfaces at age x and in the year y:

$$\ln m_{x,y} = \beta_0 + \beta_1 X$$

(A.11)

where X is the dummy variable equal to 0 for the first population and 1 for the second one. Parameter estimates of an analytic form can easily be found:

$$\hat{\beta}_0 = \ln \frac{\sum_{i,j} w_{i,j} D_{i,j}}{\sum_{i,j} w_{i,j} N_{i,j}}$$

(A.12)

$$\hat{\beta}_1 = \ln \frac{\sum_{i,j} w_{i,j} D^*_{i,j}}{\sum_{i,j} w_{i,j} N^*_{i,j}} - \hat{\beta}_0$$

(A.13)

Finally, $r_{x,y}$ is computed as $r_{x,y} = e^{\hat{\beta}_1}$. In addition, a likelihood ratio test can be performed in order to test hypothesis $\beta_1 = 0$.

Convenient choices for the kernel functions would be the Epanechnikov kernel (Appendix 5) and single-year-age kernel ($w_{i,j}$ is equal to 1 for $i = x$ and $j = y$, and 0 otherwise). In latter case $r_{x,y}$ is simply the ratio of the corresponding central death rates $r_{x,y} = \dfrac{m_{x,y}}{m^*_{x,y}}$.

Appendix Table 8.

List of causes of deaths selected for the analysis of mortality differences.

Cause	Cause of death	ICD9 BTL	ICD8 A-list	ICD7 A-List
Chapter I. Infective and parasitic diseases.				
1	Infective and parasitic diseases	B01x-07x	A1-44	A1-43
Chapter II. Malignant neoplasm.				
2	Malignant neoplasm of trachea, bronchus and lungs	B101	A51	A50
3	Malignant neoplasm of prostate	B124	A57	A54
4	Malignant neoplasm of intestine, except rectum	B092-093	A48	A47
5	Malignant neoplasm of stomach	B091	A47	A46
6	Malignant neoplasm of rectum and rectosigmoid junction	B094	A49	A48
7	Malignant neoplasm of breast	B113	A54	A51
8	Residual neoplasm	B08x-17x	A45-61	A44-60
Chapter III. Cardiovascular Diseases.				
9	Ischaemic heart disease	B27	A83	A81
10	Other forms of heart disease	B28	A84	A82
11	Cerebrovascular disease	B29	A85	A70
12	Disease of arteries, arterioles and capillaries	B300-302	A86	A85
13	Residual cardiovascular diseases	B25x-30x	A80-88	A79-86
Chapter IV. Diseases of respiratory system.				
14	Pneumonia	B321	A91-92	A89-91
15	Bronchitis, emphysema and asthma	B323-325	A93	A93
16	Influenza	B322	A90	A88
17	Residual respiratory diseases	B31x-32x	A89-96	A87-97
Chapter V. Diseases of digestive system.				
18	Cirrhosis of liver	B347	A102	A105
19	Peptic ulcer	B341	A98	A99-100
20	Residual diseases of digestive system	B33x-34x	A97-A104	A98-107
Chapter VI. Accidents, poisonings, and violence (E).				
21	Suicide and self inflicted injury	B54	A147	A148
22	Motor vehicle accidents	B471	A138	A138
23	Accidental falls	B50	A141	A141
24	Residual accidents	B47x-56x	A138-150	A138-150
Chapter VII. Residual group of diseases.				
25	Residual group of diseases			

Appendix 9. Contents of the accompanying CD-ROM.

Description	Folder
Monograph in PDF format	\Monograph
Trends in cause-specific death rates in Denmark, Sweden, the Netherlands and Japan in HTML format. To start open `cause.htm` in a web browser.	\causes
Color Lexis maps in PDF format.	\Figures
Animated figures of Danish population and mortality changes. To start open `!start.htm` in a web browser.	\Animation
Lexis software for creating contour maps oriented on demographic problems. All maps included in this monograph have been created with help of this program. The software has been created and copyrighted by Kirill Andreev. Lexis version 1.1 is distributed free of charge together with this monograph, please, cite this publication if you use it.	\Lexis
Adobe Acrobat Reader 4.00. This software is used to view PDF format files. The software has been downloaded from Adobe Web site: www.adobe.com. To install the reader double click on the program icon and follow instructions on the screen.	\ar

In the series Odense Monographs on Population Aging the following volumes have been published:

MONOGRAPHS ON POPULATION AGING

General Editors
Bernard Jeune and James W. Vaupel

Vol. 1
Development of Oldest-Old Mortality, 1950-1990:
Evidence from 28 Developed Countries
Väinö Kannisto

Vol. 2
Exceptional Longevity:
From Prehistory to the Present
Bernard Jeune and James W. Vaupel (Eds.)

Vol. 3
The Advancing Frontier of Survival:
Life Tables for Old Age
Väinö Kannisto

Vol. 4
Population Data at a Glance:
Shaded Contour Maps of Demographic Surfaces over Age and Time
James W. Vaupel, Zhenglian Wang, Kirill F. Andreev,
and Anatoli I. Yashin

Vol. 5
The Force of Mortality at Ages 80 to 120
A.R. Thatcher, V. Kannnisto, and J.W. Vaupel

Vol. 6
Validation of Exceptional Longevity
Bernard Jeune and James W. Vaupel (Eds.)

Vol. 7
Mechanisms of Aging and Mortality:
The Search for New Paradigms
Kenneth G. Manton and Anatoli I. Yashin

Vol. 8
Longevity Records:
Life spans of Mammals, Birds,
Amphibians, Reptiles, and Fish
James R. Carey and Debra S. Judge

Vol. 9
Evolution of the Danish Population
from 1835 to 2000
Kirill F. Andreev

Aging Research Center
University of Southern Denmark, Odense